Change will not come if we wait for some other person or some other time. We are the ones we've been waiting for. We are the change that we seek.

- Barack Obama

TABLE OF CONTENTS

Chapter 1

Introduction

Many of my memories of being a child growing up in the heartland of India in the 1980s are marked by waiting in every aspect of life: waiting for hours for the lights to come back from the daily power cuts; waiting in line to buy groceries and other basic necessities; to withdraw or deposit money in banks, buy a movie or a train ticket, pay monthly bills and school fees, and other daily chores. Waiting was a very accepted part in the day-to-day life in India. I always wondered why nothing seemed to work without lines and waiting.

Most of the schools I attended had a bare minimum of infrastructure – tables, chairs, and a blackboard. There were no libraries, no musical instruments or sports infrastructure such as a gym or a swimming pool, no sports equipment, or even a real playground with swings, slides, or a merry-go-round. As I moved to various schools, a few did not even have teachers for certain subjects. When we did have teachers, a number of them were not interested in teaching at all. In the sixth grade, my geography teacher took naps at 10 AM while the whole class played tag outside. In high school, rather than teaching in the class, certain teachers used school as a place to recruit students for their after-school private tuition programs. I could not understand why schools had such limited resources or why the overall quality of education was so poor.

Most of my childhood, I lived in cities of 100,000-250,000, where cycle-rickshaws were the only local mode of transport. Very few people owned a car. Everyone had to walk long distances to get to school or to run daily errands. I would sit down to watch roadside blacksmiths, potters, jewelers, and other artisans as I took breaks while walking home from school. It was always hard to see my mother carrying groceries in harsh weather as she either could not find a cycle-rickshaw, or decided not to take one as they asked an unreasonable fare. I wondered why cities did not invest in developing local transport such as buses, trams, or even an auto-rickshaw network. Most small to medium size cities in India still lack local transport infrastructure. This has resulted in an explosion of personal vehicles such as two-wheelers, and small cars even in the small cities. This has brought new problems of traffic congestion and severe pollution even to the small to medium size Indian cities.

As a child, I was horrified of out-of-town travel. As the buses always took more people than they had seats, more often than not one had to travel standing for part or the whole trip. One has to travel in India's state transport buses to really relate with the word "miserable." It seemed the seats on those buses were meant to transport prisoners. Buses were typically in poor condition and broke down frequently. In over forty-five degree Celsius unbearable heat, sometimes bus windows could not be opened for fresh air as they were stuck. The buses made terrible noise. Every time I traveled, I feared the bus could fall apart any moment like a cardboard box. Travelling on single-lane roads filled with potholes was a terrifying experience. First, you were tossed from side-to-side as the bus partly got off and back on the road to pass oncoming traffic. Then you were thrown off your seat every few minutes as the bus hit the potholes, which went on for the whole duration of the trip. I was at a loss to understand why public transport was so dreadful. Why did the bus companies not install air conditioning in such extreme hot weather?

Depositing or withdrawing your own money from a bank felt like asking someone for a favor. After I complained to the manager that he was gone from his seat for forty-five minutes for a tea break at 10 AM when there were twenty people waiting in line, a teller once refused to serve me, accusing me of moving up the line without waiting for my turn. If you needed a demand draft (equivalent to a bank check), you had to wait for hours after depositing the cash, as if they waited for someone else to show up claiming the cash you deposited for the demand draft. I questioned why the banks could not just add extra resources to make the process easier for their customers.

Anywhere you went across the country, towns looked like trashcans. Plastic bottles, paper bags, wrappers, cigarette cases, and every kind of trash could be seen everywhere. People buying food on the buses and throwing wrappers out of the window, or under their seat, was just normal behavior. There were hardly any trashcans or mechanisms for trash collection. Overflowing trash blocked city drains, and water stalled in the drains made the situation worse with horrible stink. But it hardly mattered. For weeks, everyone living on my street held their breath until they got out of the street because of the smell of stalled water and other waste. I wondered at the local government's ineffective response to the stalled city sewers, the total absence of playgrounds, the city streets filled with potholes, and the roads so narrow that accidents seemed always to be waiting around the next turn.

India has made progress over the last twenty-five years in a number of areas where the private sector has been allowed to compete. It has given hope to millions of people for a better tomorrow. But even today's India is struggling with the same basic issues of the 1980s, with the addition of new serious issues in the mix. India is still unable to provide 24/7 electricity, sanitation, or running water to millions across the country. With time, more water shortages will be faced by people everywhere in India. Power cuts in forty-five-degree heat are still common. With the explosion of personal cars, intra and intercity traffic has become a major new issue. A twenty-five kilometer trip during office hours in major cities can take hours. Widespread trash, stalled water sewers, and severe water pollution causing disease has become a national problem. India is producing masses from its education system with few employable skills, resulting in high unemployment and significant increases in the crime rate. Dramatic air pollution, lack of basic amenities like public parks, and people living in extreme poverty, are visible everywhere. Corruption in government services and social issues, such as regionalism and communalism, has grown nationally. Overall, the quality of life for poor and middle class populations has continued to deteriorate.

In the 1970s and '80s, if you asked most adults about such poor quality of life, the answer was always to blame it on the government. An average person did not seem to know how to fix these issues. By the time I was a teenager, it seemed like we were waiting for someone else to solve our problems, someone utterly apart from us, who did not live in our community, city, or even our country.

In my early twenties I came to the United States for higher education and found myself in a system where everything just worked as expected. The power was on all the time, the highways were incredible; getting a phone took merely hours; the tellers at the bank waited on you; city streets were spotless. It was incredible to get 24/7 hot and cold running water – when hot water in winters in northern India was a luxury – and every town had a local library with thousands of books. The public schoolteachers were invested in the education of their students. Every ten years, the US produced significant innovations in all aspects of human life. Everything simply worked.

I started to compare the two systems – the India of 1980s and '90s and the United States that I now called home. Both countries are rich in natural resources. Both countries are democratic, and their citizens share a desire for good living conditions and better lives for the next generation. The United States is widely regarded as the envy of the rest of the world, whereas India seems to stagnate in mediocrity despite having all the potential.

On paper, India actually seemed to be better situated to succeed. India has a much older cultural history, as well as the force of youth on its side. Sixty-five percent of India's population is below thirty-five. India's geographical location, even with rudimentary tools, allows it to produce food for its over one billion population. India's trained scientists, engineers, business professionals, and even blue-collar workers have proved themselves to be some of the best. Yet at the same time, India is not only struggling to feed its people and produce enough jobs for its youth, but it ranks at the bottom of any kind of measure around the world. India has really not provided any significant contribution in the progress of humankind over the last thousand years.

Since both systems share similar sets of values and expectations, it is the policies enacted at the local, state, and national level that has allowed one system to excel while the other rots from the inside out.

Waiting For Us looks at India's problems from the inside out. It raises an alarm that if the problems are not fixed at the fundamental level, India, as we know today may not exist as a country in the next twenty-five years.

India was never a country until Mughals and later the British united it and ruled it as one country. Indian states were run by dictatorships, where the majority of the population was poor and ruled by ruthless rulers. Even though there was a huge diversity of language, customs, food, and even gods, all these people did not want to go back to any kind of dictatorship of the last 2,000 years. They all came together to build a just, democratic and prosperous country. Today, that hypothesis is challenged. Unrest in Kashmir, extreme poverty in eastern states, high unemployment and poverty across the majority of India's population, and increasing crime, makes for a perfect storm for its people and states to go on their own way.

Waiting For Us analyzes how all of India's problems are inter-related and can only be solved by implementing a large policy framework. *Waiting For Us* lays out such a policy framework, and recommends certain key reforms. India needs changes at all levels, including constitutional changes like limiting terms of elected and nominated politicians, removing non-confidence motions and other major changes to the Indian constitution, smaller and transparent government acting as a referee and allowing the private sector to lead industry. *Waiting For Us* discusses how the government's main focus should be to implement reforms across all aspects of industry, education, environment, law and order, and national security, which impact daily lives of all Indian people. It also identifies common sense solutions already deployed around the world to similar problems to improve the day-to-day life of millions of people living in India.

Waiting For Us shows how privatizing industries such as railways, garbage collection, and recycling will not only make life easier for the masses and clean up the cities, it outlines how it privatizing will also create millions of new jobs. It suggests ways to wean India's economy from oil and coal to renewable energy sources developed and managed by the private industry. Not only will such transformation will bring 24/7 power India needs, it will also reduce the pollution choking India's cities, and create hundreds of thousands of new jobs. The book suggests a policy framework to make tourism a $100 billion revenue generator, and to transform India into the world's hospital by allowing private enterprise to build and manage healthcare under government oversight, making it a trillion dollar business, creating millions of new jobs India's youth needs today.

Waiting For Us advocates getting government out of major industry by selling their stock to public so these companies cannot keep on coming back to the taxpayers every year to bail them out. At the same time, the policy framework requires that the privatization or creation of these large industries be done transparently without politicians assigning the contracts to their friends and family and holding the private industry accountable for its actions.

Waiting For Us proposes an education policy framework to improve access and quality of education at every level. A well-educated population not only adds to overall GDP, it helps in building a better society, helps to elect the most qualified leaders, who questions its government and keeps them honest to do their jobs.

Waiting For Us provides a platform to anyone who believes in the same approach to solving India's problem to speak up and ask these policies to be implemented in their local, state, and the national government. Using *Waiting For Us* as a platform, the book encourages citizens to get involved politically to promote and implement its policies, to challenge political parties promoting division based on race, religion, and caste, putting all of India's citizens, and its next generations, in great peril, threatening India's future as a country in the long run.

Finally, at the outset, it may sound daunting to bring the policy changes *Waiting For Us* proposes. Some changes may sound counterintuitive and against the self-interest of India's power centers, who are in charge of bringing about these changes as such changes will take money and power away from them.

Unfortunately, India has reached a tipping point. We all breathe the same air, drive the same roads, are exposed to the same diseases, and have the same probability of becoming a victim of random crime outside of our homes. It is in everyone's interest to make these policy changes for their children and their grandchildren's future. Failure to act will have equally catastrophic consequences to all, irrespective of their caste, religion, position, power, money and profession.

Let's get started. India is *Waiting For Us*, the common people, to act for the India We Deserve!

Chapter 2

Role of Government

In my analysis, India's failure up to the 1980s can be attributed to four key points. First, government controlled economy; second, lack of campaign finance laws to fund its elections; three, government's caste-based reservations in higher education and jobs; and four, government-approved license raj.

Government Controlled Economy:

One of my key observations of 1980s India is that government was omnipresent in the average citizen's day-to-day life. One could not do anything without interacting with government departments or employees. Government was the largest employer. Government ran everything required in day-to-day life such as schools and universities, banks, transportation—including gas stations, buses, and trains—telecommunications, radio and television, water, garbage collection, roads and highway construction and maintenance, ports, rivers, dams and canals, hospitals, defense, police and fire department, power generation and distribution and airlines. Government also ran all heavy manufacturing including oil and gas production and distribution, mining, metal production plants, cement, manufacturing of turbines, planes, space technology and development, and all other heavy manufacturing. Through subsidies to farmers for power, seeds and fertilizers and also setting up wholesale market pricing, the government even controlled India's overall food supply.

Government jobs provided complete job security. Annual raises and promotions were based on seniority and not on job performance. As an example, one of my neighbors who worked in a public works department typically left for his office around noon and left the office at five in the evening. For him, a three-hour workday was justified for the money he was paid to do his job. He also knew there would be no consequence for showing up only for part of the day. This forced the whole system to slowly break down over time, creating a culture of lines and waiting.

In the government-run schools, low salaries for school administrators and teachers resulted in out-of-date curricula and poor teaching methods, and ultimately produced a large number of students unprepared to compete in the real world. In reality, a large number of teachers went into the teaching profession because of the employment guarantee it provided. Even if some teachers wanted to do their job, it was hard. Class sizes of 50-80, classrooms with minimal infrastructure, harsh working conditions—the number of times the fans did not work in unbearable heat between March and May, and labs with minimal supplies, did not help in keeping their morale up. This had major consequences at the national level. For thirty years, schools churned out students with not much knowledge but a certificate. Additionally, millions of children did not even have access to schools. It was not uncommon to find that a few of my classmates walked miles to attend school, as that was the closest school to their village. That resulted in high illiteracy rates. High illiteracy rates played a major role in India's population explosion from the 1950s to the 1980s.

Municipal government, charged with keeping towns and cities clean, were not any different: lack of infrastructure to recycle or dispose of trash, no real tools except brooms and shovels, employees with guaranteed jobs with low salaries who either could not keep up or were not motivated enough to do their jobs—resulting in towns looking like trashcans. Unfortunately, it has continued to be the same even today.

Government job guarantees and low salaries coupled with the population explosion was also the recipe for poor quality of customer service across all service sectors run by the government. Typically, a few government personnel were assigned per thousands of customers for any government service. On government-run railways, which transported millions of people across the country: 1:1000-10,000 agents-to-travelers ratios were the reality of daily life. Similarly, bus stations, utilities companies, schools, and government-run banks and hospitals, usually had only a handful of resources serving tens of thousands of people, resulting in long lines and poor service. Given that it was purely up to the employee to show up to work if they felt like it, with no consequences if they didn't, people stood in lines to get a train ticket or pay a bill and waited for hours.

Guaranteed jobs and low salaries enabled retail level corruption to seep in at the most basic levels. Bureaucrats and other government employees who dealt with citizens directly used their positions to enrich themselves through delaying work, or just outright denying something unless they were bribed. Each activity where government employees were in charge of activities which touched people's day-to-day life became fair game for corruption: opening a bank account, getting business permits, a phone connection, a housing permit, avoiding a traffic ticket, lowering the meter reading for electric and water bills, admissions in schools, getting cement to build a house, or getting a transfer or stopping a transfer in a government job.

Even in schools corruption took roots. I had friends who boasted gifting alcohol to a teacher to get perfect grades in labs. One of my earliest memories of corruption is a traffic cop stopping every truck crossing an intersection, boarding the truck, and then getting off at the other side of the turn. With government running most industries, jobs resulted in poor service and corruption in every aspect of daily life.

The government-run economy basically inhibited all innovation and stalled progress for decades when other countries made dramatic progress in an open market economy.

Lack of Campaign Finance Laws to Fund its Elections:

Corruption was further fueled dramatically due to lack of appropriate campaign finance laws in India. After India's independence, India's economy was run by politicians as owners and bureaucrats working as managers of the large government enterprise. Government's annual budget was allocated by the politicians, which were then passed on to various government agencies run by the bureaucrats. Politicians instructed the government bureaucrats to pay a certain percentage of the money back to the politicians to fund their political parties and elections illegally as India did not really have any campaign finance laws to fund political activity. Surely, politicians kept part of that money to build personal assets and wealth. This unfortunately continues to be common even today.

Lack of Campaign finance laws forced politicians to siphon money from large government infrastructure projects. Bureaucrats, given their jobs were in the hands of the politicians, dutifully took more money out of the system than asked by the politicians and enriched themselves in the process. Every government employee —part of the process benefited from the scheme: cashiers who made the payments, clerks who forged the expenses, quality checkers who falsified the quality reports and the officers who singed off on the whole operations made large sums of money through such corruption. These government employees became tools to redistribute the majority of India's national budget between its politicians and the bureaucrats. Less than 50% of the money assigned for any project went towards the project. The government bureaucracy and its politicians at all levels stole the rest. Any bureaucrat who did not play the game was either transferred to a remote places with almost no infrastructure, including schools, transportation, security services, or health services, or were pushed out of the system by falsely charging them with corruption or some fabricated excuse, which then forced them to entangle themselves in India's never ending and equally corrupt legal system. That was a lesson to others not to get in the way of the great get-rich-scheme. I saw this firsthand as my best friend's father was suspended as he refused to be part of the corruption game. For the next four years, his family went through hell to prove his innocence, with dramatic financial hardship and stigma. Even though he was cleared of all charges, it was surely a lesson to everyone to play the game as instructed from the top.

As a result, modern inter-state highways were never built, city infrastructure was never properly maintained, government-run transport departments ran dilapidated buses and trains and none of the government run industry whether building a turbine or a light aircraft or metallurgical plants produced a quality product thereby keeping India from becoming a first world country.

Government's Caste Based Reservations in Higher Education and Jobs:

Over time, government-run systems were further weakened due to government's policy of reservations for people of lower castes. Government policy of reservations allowed a large section of society who were repressed over the centuries based on the Indian caste system to gain admissions into government-run higher education institutions and government jobs based on caste rather than merit.

In high school, one of my next-door-neighbor families was beneficiary of the caste-based reservation system. Being a lower cast, my classmate was guaranteed admission into a government-funded college if he just showed up to write the state competitive exam. To be selected through the same exam, I had to prepare for four years studying for sixteen hours a day. When folks like me were toiling away in a mosquito-infested city in 45-degree Celsius summer temperatures studying under a kerosene lamp, my "reservation guaranteed" classmate enjoyed his summer breaks riding his motorcycle around town and easily got admitted into a state-funded engineering program. I had to wait another year to try again, and study harder to get into a similar government-funded engineering college. The year I was able to get admission in college through a grueling state level competitive exam, it selected 1,000 students from 100,000 applicants from the general population. The lowest rank reservation quota student scored a total of negative 36 in that exam.

Such reservation policies not only allowed unqualified students from lower castes to enter colleges, but it continued as preferential treatment in government jobs. Not only a large percentage of government jobs were reserved for lower caste applicants, they were automatically promoted in their jobs as they completed seven years of service without any consideration of performance. As a result, it effectively enabled a large part of the government's top bureaucracy to be run by the lower caste personnel rising to top of the organizations and effectively running the country. It not only further demoralized the government bureaucracy; it showed up in every aspect of India's daily life. As a result, overall quality of life went from very hopeful at the independence of India from the British to completely hopeless in the late 1980s.

Government Approved License Raj:

During all this time India's retail economy was run by a "pseudo" private sector under what was termed "License Raj." Right after India's independence from British, government issued licenses to select few individuals to start an industry and also regulated production of these industries. Between the direct government control of major industry and services and government control of remaining private industry through the "License Raj", government effectively controlled 100% of India's economy including food, clothes, electronics, cosmetics, cement, steel, fertilizers, books and everything people purchased at the retail level. Since India's population also grew at an extremely high rate, from 330 million in 1947 to 850 million in 1990, retail level vendors with the right connections in the government bureaucracy thrived and a small middle class was created.

The retail economy was mostly a cash economy. Merchants dealt with their customers and vendors in cash, thereby easily manipulating their sales and thereby tax liability. These retail merchants were able to take advantage of lack of transparency in the government. Without a transparent system to record sales and costs, retail merchants were able to manipulate their taxes to their advantage. In a good number of cases by bribing the taxman, most of these merchants found ways to avoid paying any tax at all. This was a double-edged sword to the government treasury. This middle class benefited by using government services for almost free, and at the same time enriched themselves by paying no tax on their incomes.

I had a firsthand lesson of India's retail economy as early as seventh grade. During that summer vacation, I worked for my uncle, who had a license to sell cement. Given there were only a few government-run factories in India producing cement at that time, it was always in short supply. Typically, cement was delivered by truck, mostly late in the night, directly from a cement factory. By 4 AM the whole truck was sold at twice the tariffed price. It was just a money-minting machine. It was the best business one could find. Everyone paid in cash. After we paid the tariffed price to the government, it was all tax-free money, except we had to pay the guy who managed the licensing for cement at the district level.

All of this resulted in the broken India I grew up in. By the late 1980s, India as a country had mostly failed its citizens. Low literacy rates resulted in a massive population explosion; a top-down bureaucratic system with reservations based on caste resulted in inept bureaucracy, massive corruption, and poor infrastructure. Government ran deficits funding all the industries it operated and social services it provided to its citizens. Due to the clear inefficiencies of the system, India was always in a constant shortage of everything. Power cuts, roads with potholes, lack of libraries, poor transportation, cities full of trash, poor healthcare and other major issues. As a result of the government bureaucracy and population explosion, by the late 1980s, India had created a rich political class, a 25 million-strong entitled bureaucratic class, a 100 million-strong middle class, and 725 million people living in abject poverty.

The situation got completely out of control by the early '90s. India almost ran out of foreign reserves. Due to fear of defaulting on international debt payments, the government was forced to open a few business sectors to private enterprise. Telecommunications, automobiles, banking and software exports were the first set of industries opened up to the private market. Over the next twenty years, these business sectors contributed more to India's employment and GDP than India's overall GDP of the previous fifty years.

India must take this formula and implement it a hundred times over. India must take the government out from running the industry and allow it's best and brightest to innovate and create opportunity for the rest of India's people. India's government needs to act as a referee and focus its investment only in the areas of defense, education, law and order, immigration, environment, and developing major infrastructure. Even in these industries, government should outsource work to private enterprises and motivate them to develop the technology indigenously. This will not only provide jobs in the short run, but India will also be able to export this technology to other developing countries, producing additional jobs and growing India's overall GDP significantly in the long run.

Over the last twenty years, India has done an excellent job in promoting primary education to its masses. The same effort and reform should be employed to secondary and higher education. Today, India is producing a large number of college graduates with minimal employable skills. India must invest in turning these graduates into productive assets for the country. If provided with proper education and training, India will produce the Einsteins, Michelangelos, Steve Jobs, Michael Jordans, and Bill Gates of the twenty-first century. With its strength in numbers, India's youth is its biggest asset. India has the potential to be the biggest economy in the twenty-first century and eradicate poverty from its masses.

But with India's population still increasing at an alarming pace, combined with the impact of global warming, India is running short on time to implement the right policy decisions. India is adding close to 2 million new workers to its work force every month. Over the next twenty-five years, India will face significant challenges from population growth and global warming, with no easy or tried solutions. The increased rate of melting of Himalayan glaciers and the drying up of underground aquifers, rising sea levels, and overall hotter weather across India, will pose significant new challenges.

India has been spared catastrophic consequences as energy prices declined dramatically in the last few years. India's policy makers have been able to hide their inaction by playing financial tactics. India must implement significant policy changes at all levels to create sustainable growth in its economy and save significant pain to its population over the next few years before it is too late. India is expected to become one of the largest economies over the next twenty-five years by a number of authors, writers and journalists, but journalists and other experts have made similar predictions in the past for a number of other countries, and when things do not come through as predicted, the same journalists write about what went wrong.

In a successful democracy, a democratically elected government has seven major responsibilities towards its citizens. Most successful democracies around the world today are not only invested heavily in these roles but also spend the majority of their annual budgets in these functions.

First: government must be responsible for the education of its people so first and foremost they become productive citizens and are able to make informed decisions in electing their representatives;

Second: provide law and order as a basic right to its citizen to protect their freedoms, including freedom of speech, non-violent protest; resolve any disputes through free and fair judiciary; and basic security, which allows them to live their day-to-day life without any fear;

Third: provide national security and border protection from all foreign threats;

Four: protect resources, including water, environment, land and other shared natural resources;

Five: act as a referee and an unbiased observer that ensures all businesses are considered equal and all their business is conducted fairly;

Six: tax collection to fund government's key responsibilities;

Seven: issuance of all official identifications, including passports, drivers' licenses, and all individual and business identity/registration numbers;

1. **Government must be responsible for the education of its people so they become productive citizens and are able to make good decisions in electing their representatives.**

A high literacy rate is one of the most common characteristics of successful democracies around the world. This not only allows citizens to be able to earn a better living than from a manual job, it also equips them in building a robust democracy as an informed citizen. Today, 99% of the wealth in the world is generated by jobs either done by machines or skilled labor.

As an example, the US provides free primary and secondary education to all children living in the US. These schools provide free books; state-of-the-art school buildings equipped with air-conditioned class rooms; the best technology, including the latest computer labs, enabling access of any and all information to students; internet enabled infrastructure for teachers to communicate with students or provide lectures, assignments, test results or keeping in touch with parents; updated curriculums and the best athletic facilities, including equipment, coaches, and infrastructure such as swimming pools, stadiums, gyms, and fields for kids to participate and compete from the local to the national level.

In addition to subsidized meals and motivated teachers, schools provide opportunities for other extracurricular activities for children to become better prepared when they graduate from high school and enter the real world: music, drama, photography, athletics, fine arts, including painting and other craft activities; skilled training like automotive repair, carpentry, computer design, broadcasting, and various similar skill development courses. Basic free and mandatory primary and secondary education builds the foundation of a healthy and strong democracy. India does not need to invent this. Today there are a number of very successful primary and secondary education models in the US, Europe, and the Nordic countries. India can pick and choose and build its own model to succeed. For any democracy to succeed, it must invest in their children, as they are not only the future of that country, but also the future of the whole of mankind in an interconnected world.

Over the last twenty years, India has invested and seen strong results in its primary education. Rather than funding a $1.5 billion USD equivalent annual loss just for Air India (which 99% of India's population does not use) such funds could be used for primary and secondary education across the country. With 1.5 billion USD equivalent, and working with local business in a 50:50 public-private partnership, India can add 150,000 primary schools with a 20,000 USD equivalent annual budget per school. With a class size of forty, this could provide primary education to 6 million children across the country. Other creative ways to fund primary and secondary education must be found to bring India's literacy rate to as close as possible to one hundred percent.

Today, a leader in higher education, the US has over 2,500 universities offering four-year college degrees, and over 1,500 colleges offering two-year college diplomas. The majority of these institutes are run by non-profit organizations. A large number of students, who attend a two-year skill-based college, will go on to make the large blue-collar workforce. These workers do very well financially, and also fulfill key roles in overall society. Students attending college are helped by the government with low interest government loans, scholarships, (private and state-funded), and study-work programs. The US college system is the envy of the world, producing some of the best college graduates and building the largest GDP in the world.

Additionally, successful U.S. colleges and universities attract the world's best and brightest students from around the world to their campuses to create the next set of innovations, resulting in jobs and a higher GDP. Just in the last twenty-five years, Indian and Chinese immigrants in the US by themselves have created companies in total value higher than India's total GDP. As a result of investments made in its schools and universities, the US has produced most of the innovations in the twentieth century, resulting in the largest GDP in the world. There is no reason India could not replicate this model and lead the world in the twenty-first century. India already has an established base of colleges and universities. If nurtured properly, these universities can become a home to the best and brightest of the developing countries around the world.

India's students attending schools and universities abroad have excelled in their fields. Indian scientists, engineers, and entrepreneurs are one of the most successful ethnic groups around the world. It is India's people who have built large economies across the Middle East from nothing except their hard work. Students coming out of India's IITs, NITs, and IIMs, have achieved unparalleled results in creating wealth, jobs, and innovations when these universities do not even rank in the top one hundred universities around the world. If given the right framework, resources, and a free hand, these institutions can become the very best in the world.

For higher education institutions to compete with that of the US, Germany, and other advanced countries, India needs a substantial investment in infrastructure, which can only be achieved through private-public partnerships. Private enterprises should be invited to make investments in science and technology infrastructure. Successful professionals should be added to college and university boards to make sure that curriculums are not only up to date but are also revised frequently to keep up with the times. State and national governments should offer no-interest student loans and scholarships for India's best and brightest students to be identified and nurtured to become leaders in their fields. Sports franchises and large public enterprises should be invited to invest in college level sports to build sports infrastructure and a revenue model to develop programs and athletes to compete at the international level.

At the same time, major reform must be enacted to motivate individuals interested in teaching by revising teachers' pay annually by charging fees to students, assigning part of local government taxes to education, and private industry participation in overall education funding. Investments must be made in standards and training to help India's real wealth, its children, lead India in every sphere of life in the twenty-first century.

In the twenty-first century, an educated population is a must to eradicate poverty. India's policy makers must put education as their most important national priority, which could help not only eradicate poverty but also showcase India's way of life as described in India's *Upanishads* and *Vedas* for the rest of the world to follow.

2. Provide law and order as a basic right to its citizen to protect their freedoms, including freedom of speech, non-violent protest; resolve any disputes through a free and fair judiciary, and provide basic security which allows them to live their day-to-day life without any fear.

Successfully democracies are built on the rule of law. They protect freedom of speech, allow people to live without fear of oppression by bullies, thugs, or the government itself, allow people to resolve their disputes in a court of law, and make for a successful transition of power at every level through democratic means.

For India to be able to be successful, it must invest significantly in its legal system and its police force. Today, India has seventeen judges per million people in comparison to one hundred judges per million people in the US. For a successful democracy, government must invest significantly not only in an adequate number of judges, prosecutors, and judicial staff, it must provide state-of-the-art infrastructure, including building, computers, and other technology for the judiciary to be swift, transparent, and free of corruption. Most judicial infrastructure is dilapidated. There is hardly any use of technology found in lower courts. It takes a generation before a property dispute is resolved or a simple financial transaction is settled in a court. Assumption of corruption in the judiciary is commonplace.

Similarly, India's police personnel lack sufficient infrastructure, resources, and training. India is currently second-last in the world, employing 129 police personnel per 100,000 people. The average number of police personnel around the world per 100,000 people is 350. With a huge income gap between the rich and poor, a high population growth rate, and high unemployment, crime is already exploding in Indian cities and will become a top issue in the next decade. Today, like the judiciary, a perception of rampant corruption in India's police at all levels is commonplace. Every month, India makes international headlines with sexual assaults on women in its major cities. Indian daily newspapers are filled with petty crimes and murders mostly lost in other myriad of issues faced by people in their daily lives.

India must invest heavily in police personnel and technology, like cars, computers, high tech labs, and body cameras to create a state-of-the-art and trustworthy police force. India, a country founded on the principles of non-violence, a society whose foundation is built on following the truth, can be a moral guide to the world.

3. Provide national security and border protection from all foreign threats.

The defense of its people, and a secure border, are one of the fundamental roles of any form of government. It is the government's key responsibility to fund national defense, including an army, navy and air force. Given India's location and history with its neighbors, it is even more important for India to properly fund its defense forces and equip them with the best training and technology.

Since India's wars with its neighbors in the '60s and '70s, India has built one of the largest defense forces in the world. Today, India has the fourth largest defense budget, spending over 40 billion USD equivalent per year.

However, India purchases most of its defense technology, including airplanes, ships, radars and other weapon systems, from countries around the world. Over the years, equipping India's defense forces by technology purchased from foreign countries has resulted in two major issues. First, this has brought rampant corruption, bribery, and scandals to the Indian defense apparatus. In the last thirty years, the Indian press has reported a number of bribery cases related to purchases of helicopters, Jeeps, howitzers, trucks, and missiles purchased for billions of USD. Secondly, this takes away a large portion of the annual budget that could be used to create millions of jobs and growth in India's GDP, which India desperately needs.

First, to remove such corruption and track the money spent in India's defense industry, government should bring transparency, including technology at every step of the contract to purchase process, and put the top leadership responsible for all transactions. If any of the deals are found to have corruption or kickbacks taken by the leadership, not only should these leaders be tried and jailed, but also their party should be banned from elections for the next twenty years.

To resolve the second issue, government should build a twenty-year plan to build all of India's defense technology by Indian companies. A 40 billion USD equivalent investment in India's defense industry could produce up to 50 million new direct jobs, and another 50 million secondary jobs. Furthermore, Indian companies could then export these products to the rest of the world at a cost most developed countries could not compete with.

4. Protect resources, including water, environment, forests and other shared natural resources, and build infrastructure such as roads, bridges, highways, ports, railways, and bus station and airports.

Every citizen has a basic right to clean air, water, and sanitation in order to live a long and healthy life. It is a key role of government to protect the country's natural resources for its people today and for its future generations. Additionally, for citizens to lead meaningful and productive lives, government should be responsible for basic infrastructure such as roads, bridges, highways, canals and waterways, ports and airports, to create businesses and services to build a strong economy and create employment.

For the last forty years, most of India's natural resources and infrastructure have been in a dramatic decline. India today has the top twenty most polluted cities in the world. Polluted air in large cities is causing significant health issues such as asthma, weak lungs, and other maladies. The large number of cars and factories releasing poisonous chemicals into the air causes most of the air pollution. Government should enact and enforce laws to protect India's environment. There are a large number of solutions used around the world's largest cities to solve the air pollution problem. In the '70s, the US enacted and enforced environmental laws for power plants and factories to use technology to solve similar pollution problems and successfully solve the air pollution problems in its major cities. At the same time, the US government enforced laws for the auto industry to adhere to air quality standards to sell cars in the US. Every few years, the US government, working with auto industry, continues to make the air standards stricter to continue to reduce pollution from the ever-increasing number of cars on the road. India must enact and enforce similar laws to reduce automobile pollution and invest in public transport to reduce the number of cars in its cities.

Not only does India have one of the most polluted rivers in the world, but also due to climate change and global warning a number of India's large rivers are drying up during the summer months. This has been catastrophic for a large section of people in India. Since over seventy percent of India's population is dependent on agriculture, such water shortages have caused high inflation of food products and high unemployment in farm workers. The dramatic decline in water supply has resulted in thousands of farmers committing suicides across the country. It has also resulted in India's major cities not being able to provide water to people living in these cities for their day-to-day use. Additionally, with no regulation on use of underground water, water tables in cities have dropped dramatically over the last twenty years. Water shortages in cities from rivers and underground resources are already a major concern for most mid to large cities. Given India's large population and global warming warnings, India must restrict use of ground water and find ways to solve the water problem before it is too late.

It is of utmost importance that the government enforces laws to stop further pollution of rivers by industry, and use solutions implemented around the world to clean up India's rivers. Global warming is an alarming problem with no simple solutions. India must use its best and brightest to find unique solutions to restore the health of rivers.

India has also lost a lot of forest cover in the last fifty years, mostly due to urbanization, wood used as a cooking fuel, and for cremation purposes. Losing forest cover has not only increased the air pollution dramatically, it has also added to irregular and reduced rainfall much needed for agriculture in India. Cities around the world are working to plant millions of trees, and laws have been enacted to stop cutting forests all together. India must pass and enforce laws to ban cutting down trees, plant millions of trees across the country, and promote electric cremation to restore India's forest cover for its current and future generations in order to start reversing its environmental health, and stabilize its much-needed rainfall.

Today, India's economy and country as a whole is held back due to its poor infrastructure. India lacks basic infrastructure such as roads and highways, airports, power distribution grids, ports, and recycling plants, to build a twenty-first century economy. India needs massive investment in its basic infrastructure at the earliest opportunity. Government should sell its stake from all businesses it runs today and invest the money in infrastructure by contracting it out to be built by the private sector. Government should be focused on building transparent processes, which can reward these contracts expeditiously with direct supervision by the top leadership of the country.

5. Act as a referee and an unbiased observer that ensures all businesses are considered equal and all their business is conducted fairly.

India's greatest successes in the last twenty years have occurred where the government has opened certain industries to private companies. Automobiles, telecommunications, information technology, and banking are only a few of the industries that have benefitted significantly from enabling private enterprise to enter these markets and compete to provide jobs and services to India's large population.

Most successful capitalistic democracies have invested time and money to make sure it is a simple and straightforward process for its citizens to start and operate a business. Government acts as referee to promote healthy competition among these businesses, and modifies and enacts new laws to protect the rights and interests of its citizens from being abused. Such a system over time produces innovation, jobs, and a social safety net for its citizens.

Even today, India's government works through decades-old processes, using paper files as it has done for the last fifty years. As a first step, India's government must mandate the use of technology in all government processes to make all these processes a lot more efficient and remove any chances of corruption by the government bureaucracy, including government contracting; essential services, ranging from driver's license, passport, or other form of identity issuance; all forms of licensing and permits required to start or run a business; tax collections; issuance of traffic violation; legal notices, and any other process where government interacts with individuals and businesses. Additionally, all accounting of government spending must be opened to the public, using technology for private citizen watchdogs to expose any corruption at all levels. Transparency through advanced technology should be made mandatory for all government department functions. Government must communicate through e-mail, and allow all data to be accessible over the Internet whenever it is feasible.

As a legislative body, government should amend and pass new laws to protect citizens' civil rights. Mandatory minimum wage, patient bill of rights, privacy protection laws, laws to prevent collusion by businesses, protection of civil liberties, and all other rights to protect citizens must be enacted or modified by the government to act as a referee and unbiased arbitrator for society.

6. Tax collection to fund Government Key Responsibilities.

Only a very small fraction of people pays any taxes in India today. As a result, India's government is unable to fund its key responsibilities such as infrastructure, funding of law and order, protection of environment, and other social services expected from government. Today, India's large middle class is able to avoid paying any taxes because they are able to manipulate their incomes. Currently, retail businesses are not required to track sales and payments electronically.

It can only be fixed by mandatory enforcement of technology at the retail level. Most small to medium size businesses are proprietary firms. To makes sure that such businesses are not able to manipulate their income and expenses by doing cash transactions, they must be required to use technology to track all transactions. Implementation of such basic steps is enforced around the world.

Tax collection should also be made simple. Today, an average person cannot file taxes on their own due to complexities of the tax filing process. For a large number of people, it is more expensive to file a tax return than the tax they owe. Tax forms and filing should be simplified to a level of mailing a postcard.

At the same time, all income tax departments must be computerized and all inquiries, returns, and communications originating from income tax departments must have an electronic trail. This would not only bring efficiency, but would reduce corruption dramatically. Furthermore, income tax departments should remove all local contact with businesses regarding any income tax issues. Contact between local merchants and income tax personnel enable corruption and avoidance of taxes. All tax queries, submissions, and communications must be done from central locations via written or phone contacts. Government should provide funding for income tax department to hire adequate staff to process and audit income taxes from all individuals and businesses. Software programs must be introduced to audit all reporting of sales, payrolls, and expenses paid by a business to other businesses and individuals. Such technology implementation will enforce collection of tax at every level to allow government to then fund its basic responsibilities.

7. **All Immigration policy, issuance of all official identifications including passports, drivers' licenses, all individual and business identity cards.**

It is one of government's key roles to define and implement India's immigration policy. For all social services, national security, immigration, and employment services, government must issue unique and secure identifications to all of its citizens. Government should contract private companies to manufacture such physical identifications, but manage overall quality and security control.

Government must also define a firm time frame for issuance of all identifications, and each type of identification processing must be done electronically from a different central location without a direct human contact in order to eliminate any and all possibilities of fraud and corruption.

Different government agencies should be made responsible for the issuance these ID cards. For example, a stand-alone agency should be made in-charge of issuing all driver licenses, car registration, and mandating of all national traffic laws. Similarly, all passport issuance should be brought under a second agency. All employment and social benefit identifications must be managed under a third agency so that all social benefits are paid correctly. Lastly, a fourth agency, under the supervision of the tax department, must be created to issue all business identifications. At the same time, all such processing should be done electronically to reduce bureaucracy.

Chapter 3

Make Key Changes Now: Before it is Too Late Constitutional Changes | Education Reform | Law & Order | Legal Reform

Before one plans an expedition of any kind, one has to follow a process. First, you need functioning transportation. Once you have arranged transportation, you must know how to drive or arrange for a driver. You must also know the traffic rules and directions to get to your destination. You will have to make arrangements to stay in a hotel and do research for places to visit to make your vacation a success. But none of it is possible unless you have a functioning transport.

Similarly, for a democratic society to function, it needs four key pieces to be in place before other functions can be planned and successfully executed. Here are the four key pillars needed to build a successful democracy:

1. A living constitution, one that evolves, changes over time, and adapts to new circumstances;
2. Education: for democracy to thrive and democratic institutions to function, a well-educated population is a must.
3. A strong and transparent law and order system.
4. An efficient and well-regarded legal system that enables people to resolve their disputes in a timely manner and which protects average citizens from the rich and powerful.

First and foremost, India must critically examine its constitution, which was borrowed from nineteenth and twentieth century Europe and communist Soviet Union. Some of India's constitutional structure, in addition to stymieing India, has failed across Europe and also brought down the Soviet Union in the 1990s. India needs to take a detailed look at the aspects of its citizens' daily lives and either innovate appropriate solutions or adopt solutions developed around the world that suit its ways.

Without the right educational institutions in place, it is impossible to find an educated and skilled labor force to create wealth in the twenty-first century. Similarly, without transparent law and order and a legal system, none of the other reforms are possible in a democratic society. These four institutions must be constantly improved, and their integrity should be protected.

India's government still continues to run a large part of its industry even though there is really no need for India's government to run massive money-losing behemoths such as HAL, BHEL, NTPC, SAIL, SBI, Air India, Indian Airlines, and a number of other such companies. The success that India has enjoyed in the last twenty years can be traced to four industries that were unshackled from the government's controlling grip: banking, telecommunications, automobiles, and the IT industry. The results of privatizing these industries and limiting power of the government to that of a referee in these industries have been impressive. These advances have shown the world what India and Indians can do.

Since the 1990s, every elected government has agreed to get the government out of industrial production and large service industries, but has lacked the tools to deal with its aftermath. For any policy maker to be brave and implement these changes effectively requires a free hand. These reforms are not popular and will require making tough decisions. When and if an organization is turned into a for-profit company, management's first and foremost responsibility is to generate profit. To turn these large government-run entities into profit-making ventures, new management will have to start with laying off any redundant employees and reducing other costs to make the company profitable. In a country like India where government employs over 30 million people across every industrial and service sector, no politician or policy makers will dare take such controversial action until they are given a free hand to do so. The minute any elected government proposes privatization, most employees will force labor strikes, as the employees in these companies know that such a policy will remove millions of jobs across these industries. In today's political structure in India, any government who takes such actions will see major defection in its ranks, and the government will be ousted in a "non-confidence motion." So to save 5-10 million jobs across the inefficient government controlled industries, India continues to punish its 1 billion strong population with sub-standard products, minimal job growth, poor infrastructure, non-existent social services, and abject poverty for hundreds of millions of its people.

Constitutional Reform

For any Indian government or policy maker to unshackle India's potential, India must start with five major constitutional changes that will allow elected politicians and policy makers to initiate changes in the government.

1. Ability of the political party with most seats in an election to form a government for the full term.

2. All candidates must be local and let the contesting parties declare their chief minster or prime minster and other key leaders before elections.

3. Remove non-confidence motion from the constitution.

4. Allow anyone to be nominated as a cabinet minister.

5. Add term limits to all elected representatives.

1. Ability of the political party with most seats in an election to form a government for the full term.

India being such a diverse country, where language, food, clothes, and even the gods change within every 300 kilometers, it is amazing that one single political party governed India for the first fifty years after independence due to the high illiteracy rates among India's population. Since the early 2000s, India has seen a number of coalition national governments made up by two or more political parties, as no single political party was able to get a majority in the elections. Such alliances are made mostly to gain power. It is not unusual that on a large number of issues these political groups are 180 degrees opposed to each other's governing philosophy. It is almost comical to see that a political group that opposes almost every policy of a governing party becomes a coalition partner of the same governing party in the next election.

As a result, once these parties win an election, governing is nothing but finding ways to siphon money for personal and political gain. Each of these successive governments has really not much to show except more corruption, illogical policies, and leaving the country worse each time after they were elected at the state and the national level.

First, the governing party makes sure that it keeps its coalition partners happy by offering them certain ministries in the government so that all parties and their leaders can make money for their lifetimes, and have enough money in their coffers to fund their next election. Such corruption is clearly evident by the fact that a large number of India's politicians have achieved substantial wealth and assets during their political careers when their official salaries are substantially less and do not allow accumulation of such wealth. The time these governments have in office is spent in announcing political stunts, providing free laptops, free or subsidized food, or giving government contracts to their friends and family or coalition partners. It is impossible to get any good policy passed when the governing party is partnered with a group who is fundamentally opposed to their approach to solve major problems and also has the power to bring the government down.

Over the last twenty years, India has seen a number of coalition governments come and go at the state and national levels, most not able to serve their full terms due to non-confidence motions by a faction either lured away from the coalition by another party offering a better deal, or driven away when their policy differences were exposed. Every time, the next government unearths a number of corruption cases where the coalition partners together were stealing money for their own benefits.

To solve such a major issue, whichever party gets the most seats (even if a majority is not achieved by any party) should be allowed to form the government to get a free hand in making policy decisions for a full five-year term. Government should only be dissolved for a new election in the case of proven illegal activities. With this change, all parties out of the government will work as hawks to make sure any illegal activity by the government is reported to the public and investigated—rather than a number of political parties working in cahoots to enrich themselves.

Critics may argue that such a system has its disadvantages, that if the governing party does not have a majority it will not be able to pass any laws and will be unable to make any difference. Here the counter-argument is that once such a system is in place, parties will work together to get things done as any one of these parties could be in the same situation next time around when they would need similar help to get things done. It is still possible that "legal" favors may be exchanged between parties, but in the long run policy makers will be able to implement policies to solve day-to-day life issues without fear of losing their jobs because of the power of the coalition partner to bring a coalition government down if they are not happy with opportunities to make money for themselves, or they are fundamentally against all policies proposed by the government.

2. All candidates must be local and let the contesting parties declare their chief minster or prime minster and other leaders before elections.

India's constitution allows a person to contest an election from a constituency without even being a resident of that city, area, or even state. How can a person in a country as diverse as India relate or communicate to its local residents when they have never lived or do not even plan to live locally during their elected term? Furthermore, once the election is over, it is fairly usual for residents to hardly see their representative during their term. Residency requirements must be changed to require that only a person who's lived locally for at least two years over the last five should be able to contest elections for a constituency.

To make sure able politicians are selected to run India, political parties must be asked to declare their candidates for chief minister or prime minister and other key leaders prior to elections. Once such candidates are declared, press and citizens can understand their vision and policies for the state or the country rather than voting for hollow themes of magically eradicating poverty or voting based on religious, regional, or caste-based politics. Such a system will force parties and candidates to ask for votes based on policy, and the changes they will bring when they are elected. It will also help voters to ask questions about their issues before they vote for the candidates rather than voting for a party.

Today, if a party wins an election without declaring a leader and allows inexperienced or unsuitable individuals into government leadership (e.g. father appointing his son or daughter to become chief minister or prime minster), there is nothing people can do during that term of the government. They have to wait until the next election to remove them from the government to punish them for nepotism or other internal political schemes of the government. Such policies are commonplace and have been hurtful to India's progress.

Along the same lines, leadership should be barred from hiring direct relatives in any part of the government or doing business with the government. Such practices are commonplace today and act as a channel for politicians to funnel money to themselves. India's politicians represent the top 1% of the richest individuals in the country due to such loopholes, gaming the system or outright stealing money.

3. Remove Non-Confidence Motion from the constitution.

A group of elected members in state assembly or national parliament can bring a non-confidence motion if a majority of elected officials do not support the government. If a government cannot prove they hold the confidence of the majority of elected members, then that government has to be dissolved and a new government formed who has the approval of the majority of the elected members. Such a rule is disastrous for the common people, as any time in a coalition government, groups who support a government with a different ideology can easily hijack the effectiveness of the state or the national government, keeping government leaders hostage. As long as the non-confidence motion remains an option, government machinery is vulnerable to be ransomed by the elected members of the governing party for favors in return for their votes. Any group of party members can demand the government divert projects to their districts, ask for pet schemes to be implemented, ask for appointments in key government bureaucratic positions, get bribed through third party contractors, and collude with the government in diverting funds for personal gains.

Shutting down the non-confidence motion loophole in India's political system will have an immediate and long lasting impact on

India's policymaking benefits. This will allow the elected government (who has clearly put out their ideology before contesting an election) to implement policies they have identified and are willing to implement without any fear of non-confidence motion by the other elected members outside of the government.

4. Allow anyone to be nominated as a cabinet minister.

Today, in all state and national governments, a cabinet minister must be either an elected representative or should become an elected representative within six months of being nominated. This rule has put a chokehold on India's progress. Most qualified people in various professions do not desire to be politicians, but having spent their lifetime in a particular field, it makes them excellent candidates for cabinet minister positions to propose the right policies and remove the bad ones withholding progress in that field. The rule for only elected members to be eligible to be a cabinet ministers not only restricts the ability of the government to find the best person to promote progress in a field, in reality it guarantees frustration in the bureaucratic ranks and allows individuals to hold on to cabinet position for years— decades if the same party comes to power to form a state or a central government. It is amazing to see that today state and central governments not only keep all ministries run by a few individuals for decades rather than finding the most qualified people in a billion-plus strong population.

5. Add term-limits to all elected representatives.

The same politicians, or their sons and daughters, who were heading the state and national government in the 1990s, continue to run state and national governments today. They practically looted the government treasury and used the money to win election after election. With such a hold on the electoral process, these parties and individuals act like kings rather than elected representatives. Furthermore, they are not only able to use government infrastructure as personal property, they can carry out personal grudges against government employees who do not follow their whims.

These politicians were neither qualified nor had any desire to improve quality of life for the people they represent. Coupled with their ill-gotten wealth, it is impossible to expect this cycle to end. The only way to break this cycle is to bring term-limits to every elected position in the country. A two-term limit to every elected position, and a one-term limit to every nominated position, will bring fresh ideas and a desire to bring change at every level of society. This will also invigorate political parties themselves, as it will force them to retire older politicians and replace them with younger generations.

When India changes the constitution to allow the elected party with the most seats to assume power, allow local residents to be elected or nominated from within a constituency, removes non-confidence motions, declares leadership before an election is contested, and adds term-limits on all elected and nominated positions, India will enable its elected policy makers to exercise a free hand in implementing changes without fear of losing their position the day after their policy is introduced. Without fear of powerful politicians' ability to force personal agendas on them, such changes will also make the government bureaucracy more efficient.

This is the very first set of constitutional reforms India needs to tackle its larger problems and improve the lives of the Indian people.

Education Reform

For India to become a successful democracy, a world leader, and one of the largest economies in the twenty-first century, India must have an educated population. An educated population is key to creating jobs, building the thriving economy needed to sustain a large population, and ultimately to elect politicians and policy makers to pass intelligent laws and policies. Education reform is indisputably the most important policy for India, whose majority population is below twenty-five years in age.

Over the last twenty years, India has made tremendous progress in opening new primary schools. Unfortunately, India's primary and secondary schools continue to produce sub-par students. According to a 2016 international report, a third of India's primary school students and almost half of secondary school students drop out before completing their education. India's schools still lack basic infrastructure like toilets, books, and teachers. For schools to be able to reduce dropout rates and improve quality of education, India must allocate more resources in school infrastructure, teacher training, and programs such as reduced cost meals.

The US currently spends 7.3% of its GDP on primary and secondary education, with $11,000 per student in primary schools and $12,000 per student in secondary schools. In comparison, India spends 3% of its GDP on education and approximately $2,500 per student per year. Nearly 35% of India's population is below fourteen years old. For India to catch up with the rest of the world, India should plan to spend up to 15% of its GDP on primary and secondary education to compete with students around the world.

With the infusion of these resources, India must invest in infrastructure such as state-of-the-art schools; technology, including computers and mobile devices; internet connectivity; teaching aids; free books; subsidized lunch programs; and sports infrastructure, equipment, and training. India also must invest in teacher education and student assessment at all school levels. A major investment must be made in the review of curriculums both at primary and secondary education. In primary schools, children's bags weigh more than the students themselves. Primary education curriculum should be focused on children becoming curious and motivated to learn and pursue knowledge rather than remembering facts. Schools must remove grading in all of primary education.

Similarly, secondary education curriculums should be focused on motivating students to learn, and helping them to find their talents and areas of interest they want to pursue. Today, India's secondary schools have become a race to get the highest scores to get into government-funded colleges. Millions of students coming out of secondary schools are pursuing higher education in subjects where they may even not be interested in pursuing a career at all. Such a system is producing a large number of students graduating from government and private business, engineering and medical colleges. Most of these students are unable to find employment either due to lack of real subject knowledge and training in their respective subjects, or lack of interest in pursuing employment in that field.

Over the last fifty years, India has not produced any innovations in basic sciences, has produced very few literary works of recognition at the international level, has introduced no musicians, athletes, artisans, architects, mathematicians, city planners, software architects, fashion designers, chefs etc., who are recognized at the international level as the best of their professions. Students in secondary level should be allowed to explore and evaluate if they have interests and talents in all these subjects and fields. The secondary school curriculum should allow students to learn more about the various professions available to them once they finish high school. Higher education should allow them to get the right training for them to then pursue that profession.

Today, the majority of students graduating from higher education institutes and colleges in India are non-employable. For the last fifty years, India has glamorized engineering and medicine as top professions. Right after India's independence, government created and fully funded the Indian Institute of Technology, and a number of colleges for engineering and medicine in each state to promote these two professions. Students are selected through highly competitive state and national level entrance exams. Interestingly, a large number of students from government-funded schools leave the country to pursue education in Western countries and settle overseas. India is then left with its second and third tier of talent to advance its own engineering and medical fields. So, over the last fifty years, India has built a great system to identify and train its best and brightest minds at the Indian taxpayers' expense and help build the other economies of the Western world.

All other areas of education such as liberal arts, law, basic sciences, mathematics, music, sports, and numerous other fields, are not pursued by students due to lack of funding and recognition. For India to build a twenty-first century economy, its higher education model has to be changed dramatically. All fields and professions must be funded and recognized equally right from secondary school. Government, with private public partnerships, should fund colleges in various other fields as it has done for engineering and medicine over the last fifty years. Such private-public partnerships should allow for the opening of thousands of colleges and vocational programs, training students in all established fields like liberal arts, basic sciences, mathematics, as well as skill-based programs such as carpentry, electrician, masonry, automotive repair, nursing, customer service, hospitality, and other similar skill-based programs with equal emphasis as is done in engineering and medicine today.

Over the last few years, education has become the new booming business in India. Television ads for private schools offering primary and secondary education, and new universities offering mostly engineering educations, are omnipresent. However, the business of education in these institutes is really absent. As a policy, government should not approve any new technical institutes until the number of institutes offering liberal arts, law, and basic sciences catch up to the number of technical institutes. Alternatively, a new institute must offer multiple disciplines, including technical and non-technical subjects.

These institutes must be reviewed quarterly by a government agency. A clear standards policy should be established for all private and government-funded institutes to be evaluated by independent parties, and an annual report detailing resources, facilities, graduation rates, student grades, and the placement percentage of the graduating class should be published by the agency.

All government-funded colleges should be required to build partnerships with industry to help keep the curriculum in sync with market requirements. Government colleges should be allowed to raise funds in partnership with private companies, and government funding must be calculated based on the colleges' overall performance, graduation rates, student grades, and the placement percentage of the graduating class. In case government colleges fall below certain thresholds in student grades, teacher performance, graduation rates, or student placement, the colleges should be placed on 1-3 years probation. If the colleges are not able to improve their scores, government funding should be reduced unless the college is able to achieve the required threshold.

In summary, education policy reforms and its successful implementation must be India's top policy priority. Without the right education policy, India will find itself lagging behind in comparison to other successful economies around the world. With the right education policy, India with its young population will not only thrive but will also become the most prosperous and successful nation of the twenty-first century.

Law and Order Reform

A democratic state cannot function without a transparent and just law and order system. A law and order system consists of local, state, and national police forces, and a legal system protecting the rights of citizens.

India's current police system is outdated, too centralized, and a complete misfit for the India of today. India's police are still running under the 1865 framework created by the British, with very few modifications. Today, IPS officers selected through the Indian Civil Services exams manage the country's overall police force.

As a starter, India needs to modernize its police force with the latest technology, provide extensive training to its personnel, and decentralize the whole police infrastructure. Policing is a local issue. Police hiring decisions should be made at the city level. Mayors should be allowed to hire or fire a police chief rather than waiting for a state bureaucracy to review each policing decision of a state with hundreds of millions of citizens. Mayors know their cities and communities better than someone sitting in a state or national capital. Their citizens much more easily approach them when a problem arises. States should have a right to take over a police force for certain time intervals for well-defined reasons if such intervention is required.

State government should take up the training required for policing, as such an investment can be made in a few centers rather than replicating it in every city. State and national police commissions should provide standards and technology to provide interoperability and sharing of information between city, state, and national levels. Police personnel patrolling by foot, or bicycles, or cars should have access to the latest crime data, and all violations through mobile technology for them to make on-the-spot decisions. Police bicycles and cars should also be equipped with cameras to reduce any and all misuses of police authority. Similarly, all traffic police personnel should wear on-body cameras to make sure they do not let people go after taking money for violations.

Today, India's police are known for corruption. There seems to be a simple expectation for police personnel to be paid if they come to attend a complaint or crime irrespective if the complaint may not even have any basis. Today, India employs 138 police personnel for every 100,000 citizens. This is the fifth lowest in countries that report such data. As a comparison, the US employs 284 police personnel per 100,000 citizens. Since India is also much more densely populated, India must find the right balance to hire more police personnel to reduce crime and provide security for its people.

State and national commissions should review the police personnel recruitment and promotion process every five years across the country. All positive practices should then be implemented nationally. Similarly, poor practices should be eliminated. Police officer qualifications should be reviewed. A bachelor's degree must be required to enter a police force, as it will bring professionalism. Technology should be deeply integrated in reviewing police personnel actions and performance on a quarterly basis. Support staff at the state and national level should be tasked to monitor all police personnel across the state and country. Promotions should be made performance-based against others in their departments. Such promotion authorization decisions should be made locally with the help of data collected by the state agencies.

State and national police agencies should recommend pay scales by city, district, and regional levels based on cost of living and ranks within the department. Police personnel jobs should be at the top of any government job's pay scales as they risk their lives every day. These pay scales should be revised every year with adjustments for cost of living. Similarly, monetary awards must be given for any and all personnel involved in mishaps while on duty.

State and national police commissions should invest in crime labs equipped with the latest technologies to assist police in resolving criminal cases, and not only remove the burden from the local police but also help local police by not investing in such technologies at every local police station.

As part of overall tax reform in India, all revenues collected from traffic violations, and part of local taxes, should go to supporting local police infrastructure. This could be police buildings, experimental technology such as wearable cameras, police protection equipment such as Tasers, bulletproof vests, sprays, two-way radios, or any other new experimentation technologies that can then be used across other police departments in other districts and states.

Local police departments should also be able to use this money to reach out to local communities to build better relationships between police and the communities they serve, as well as to recruit local youth to become interested in a job in law enforcement.

Lastly, state and national police commissions should be tasked to reduce any illegal weapons, including guns, across the country, ultimately making local police jobs easier.

Legal System Reform

A democracy is a society built on the rule of law, which protects the rights of its citizens, enables law and order, limits the power of government, and whose laws are fair, impartial, and independent of government influence. By this definition, India is a democracy, but in reality India's legal system has failed India in the last thirty years.

A brief visit to any court in India will reveal everything that is wrong with India's legal system: dilapidated buildings and temporary benches that serve as offices for lawyers. Stalled water and trash strewn everywhere, that's the sad state of India's law infrastructure today. Even though infrastructure is poor in general everywhere in India, to see one of the key branches of government in such decay is sad and shocking.

India, with a population of over 1 billion, has 18 judges per 1 million people. Today there are over 27 million cases pending in the Indian legal system. Six million of these cases are over five years old. According to the chief justice of India, India needs 70,000 judges at the earliest to clear up the caseloads, versus the 16,000 judges India has today. It can take years to resolve a simple dispute through the courts. Property disputes between family members can take up a generation to get resolved. Rent laws are written in the favor of tenants, which forces property owners to rent their properties without written contracts. There have been cases where courts awarded properties to tenants who lived in a house over a long time. Since cases can take long time to resolve, property owners are hesitant to give rental contracts to tenants. This has major impacts for Indian business. Employees are unable to prove residence, which can hinder opening bank accounts or receiving other benefits.

Employment laws are typically written in favor of employees. As an extreme example, where an employee has stolen money, it is the company's responsibility to locate the employee and serve a notice. The employee can refuse to take the notice, or pay a bribe to the postman or courier to write that the notice could not be delivered, or even does not live there anymore. The company has to then put an ad in the newspaper to see if anyone can locate the person. If no response is received, the court can then ask the police to put a warrant out for that employee. At that juncture, the court may award the case to the employer. But it is still the employer's onus to collect that money by finding out a bank account number for money to be collected. A nation with such procedures cannot have the confidence of its people to become entrepreneurs and start businesses.

Laws meant to regulate daily life, including traffic laws, are a mockery of the legal system. No one follows traffic laws, including speed limits, lane merging laws, or turn signals. It is not uncommon to see people traveling in the wrong direction on a one-way street. On highways one can find cows, bicycles, scooters, cars, buses, and trucks traveling on roads without any notion of traffic rules. It is common practice to pay a bribe to a police officer when involved in minor accidents or other traffic law offenses. Driver's license infractions, including possession of a fake or expired license, or a lack of a license altogether, or driving under the influence, are all easier to pay off by bribing a traffic cop and avoiding a mark on your driving record and a court date.

Criminal laws are in a different class altogether. It is obvious that when half of the members of parliament and the legislative assembly have been charged with murder, rape, and extortion, and still retain their positions in India's most prestigious public offices, enforcement of criminal laws is not a priority. Additionally, with rising unemployment and disparity between rich and poor, crime continues to increase in India.

In order for India to become a leading economy and an example of progress in the world, the country must review, reform, and finance its legal system. Legislation must be drafted to limit the time frame in which cases must be resolved. Investments in hiring judges and legal staff, in infrastructure—including buildings and technology—are urgently needed to build trust in India's legal system.

Property, criminal, employment, and corporate laws must be reviewed and reformed as quickly as possible. This will enable entrepreneurs to bring their ideas to the market quickly, protect their intellectual property, fairly hire employees, and recoup losses in cases of theft, enforcement of employment, and other contractual obligations.

Traffic laws must be enforced properly if the Indian people are to live in a civilized system. Traffic courts must be made separate from the legal system, and must enforce quick resolutions for all traffic cases. Funds collected from fines and law enforcement could be put towards covering partial costs of traffic cases, as well as traffic police salaries and other policing costs.

A democratic country can only thrive when its judiciary system is functioning at the highest level possible. For India to achieve its potential, legal reform must be implemented immediately. Without reform, India's legal system will continue to decline and will not only impact generations to come but will also hinder any and all progress in all aspects of the economy and the daily lives of millions of India's citizens.

Chapter 4

Liberalize Now – Time is Running Out!

Over the last fifty years, each of India's successive national and state governments has introduced pet schemes to reduce poverty and offer handouts to take care of India's poor. A few state governments have offered free rice to millions of its citizens. Recently the state government of Delhi offered free or subsidized water delivered by tankers to homes. And all national governments have continued to offer free electricity and other major subsidies to farmers. Some of them are well intentioned, but most of these programs are focused to generate votes for the party in power. None of these governments has really worked to identify and resolve the issue of poverty at the core. In offering these handouts, all these governments have acted as if the country has unlimited money. The only way a government can offer services and any other assistance for free is either by taxing its citizens or taking on debt to pay for these services or any such resources. Debt is very expensive. Not only does it create a constant interest payment to be paid, it can put a country in serious jeopardy, creating dependence to the debt providers.

Today, India needs to modernize its defense, police and legal infrastructure, build and upgrade its transport and education infrastructure and clean up pollution from land, environment and rivers requiring financial resources over 2 trillion USD equivalent that India's government simply does not have.

A country can generate money in five different ways: one, just print money; two, sell its assets to domestic or foreign entities; three, through the collection of tax revenues, provided there is enough income generated by businesses and individuals to pay taxes; four, borrow money from its citizens or foreign entities; five, by foreign and domestic investors investing in building products and services to generate additional tax revenues for the country.

A country that participates in international trade cannot decide to print money on a whim. The minute a government prints more money, the country's exchange rate in relation to other currencies changes as nothing else has changed in the country by itself. So even if a country prints money, it has to pay more to acquire goods and services from outside its borders. For example, India imports most of its petroleum products. As soon as the Indian government decides to print more money, India will have to pay more to buy US dollars, which is used as a standard currency to buy petroleum products on the world market. As soon as a country prints more money, the market adjusts to the new exchange rate. Someone who works for 100 Rupees per hour will now charge more per hour, as everything around him or her will become more expensive in the local economy. As the domestic supply of goods does not change, printing money only forces them to pay more to acquire the same goods. So printing money is not a solution to funding investment in government's basic requirements. Central bankers work all their careers to make sure that inflation stays in check, as it is the first and foremost thing that impacts the day-to-day life of all people across every cross section of the country.

As a second solution, government can sell its assets to generate revenues to then invest in infrastructure, defense, education, childcare, law and order, and environmental protection. Such assets typical include the country's wireless spectrum, oil, gas, land, and minerals rights. Unless India finds a new natural resource, India's government currently sells these assets already and there is not much more leverage at this point for India to sell to generate additional revenues. However, the Indian government does have an option to sell its ownership in state-run companies. India's government over the last seventy years has invested billions of US dollar equivalent in these companies. Government can generate significant capital by selling its ownership in state-run companies to either other private enterprises or to individuals in a stock offering to the public.

Third, the Indian government can generate revenues by creating policies by which its citizens can create value through innovation and commerce. Government can then tax the income of these businesses and its employees. This is an unlimited source of revenue for any government. Most developed countries are successful in enabling their citizens to build and sell quality products internally and to other countries to generate wealth for themselves and their country.

Four, the Indian government can borrow money from its citizens or foreign entities by offering bonds, which promise to pay the debt over time with interest. Most countries around the world borrow money to either build infrastructure or fund key projects when government does not have the ability to fund them from its tax revenues. Any borrowing by a government should be done very carefully. Typically, if a government borrows money and is unable to pay its debt on time, international markets typically force the country to devalue their currencies, thereby increasing inflation and causing pain in day-to-day life. Any borrowing done by the government must be based on a clear business plan to provide a clear return on the investment, and a back-up payment plan in case the project is unable to provide the promised return on investment.

Five, the Indian government can allow foreign companies to invest in its local companies, or start new businesses to build products to be sold to its citizens or export them to other countries. Such investments from foreign companies require that India develops clear laws for land acquisition (in case a company wants to establish a manufacturing plant); good labor laws to hire and manage employees; a good legal system to fight disputes; a strong law and order system; a stable political climate over the long term for the business investment to be justified, clear tax laws for such investments; and finally a labor pool to run that business successfully. If the government is not able to provide all of these conditions satisfactory to the foreign companies, those businesses will move to other countries that are able to provide the conditions for them to be profitable.

Today, India's government has borrowed money internally from its citizens though bond offerings. It also borrows money from external sources such as the International Monetary Fund (IMF) or World Bank, or taken credit lines from countries such as Iran to buy oil and gas on credit.

In the last thirty years, India has also tried to bring money into its economy by attracting foreign companies to invest directly in domestic projects. The automobile industry is an example. Automobile companies such as Honda, Hyundai, and Suzuki have set-up manufacturing plants in India to sell their product both to Indian consumers and to export to other countries. In the short to medium time frame, such investments are good, as these investments create employment for local populations and tax revenues for the state and national government. In the long run, this could be negative as they kill the local competition and pretty much take over the market in that industry unless the government helps the local industry with tax breaks and other basic protections for them to be able to compete.

The Indian government has to make sure that local industry is supported and nurtured against competition. Currently, the automobile industry is clearly dominated by foreign manufacturers, and government must do its part to help domestic companies to compete against these entrenched manufacturers. In the long run, as labor rates increase, these foreign companies will look for cheaper manufacturing around the world and move to those countries. India must make sure that local companies have grown to fill the gap in case that happens. There are plenty of case studies around the world for government to find the right solutions to handle such situations. But for any industry to take hold, investment is very helpful, and India must encourage these investments in all sectors. Unfortunately, Indian land laws, labor laws, tax laws, lack of ease of doing business, and lack of skilled labor, has made India unattractive for such investments, and most other sectors have been unable to attract foreign interest. India needs immediate reforms in all these areas for foreign investment to continue to grow in other sectors of industry.

According to independent estimates, India's GDP is equivalent to approximately two trillion USD. In the 2016-17 financial year, India collected 263 billion USD equivalent in taxes from all sources. As per the budget, the Indian government planned to spend 304 billion USD equivalent on all of its expenditure. Less than 5%, equivalent of 15 billion USD was allocated for all infrastructure development, including highways, power, water, sanitation, river development, and law and justice combined. This surely is much smaller than what the government requires for its various infrastructure needs. Clearly, India cannot afford to borrow the trillions of USD equivalent it needs to upgrade its infrastructure, defense, education, environmental protection and social service needs of its people, or generate money by printing the extra currency. High debt and credit in turn not only hurts the credit rating of the country, it reduces the value of the country's currency and also requires government to pay interest on the outstanding debt every year. Debt is very expensive. If this cycle is not broken, eventually countries get into a downward spiral, resulting in total chaos.

This necessitates government to then raise money from other ways than discussed above. Only prudent way to generate the capital India needs is by divesting government ownership in large companies it runs. Since government has invested billions of USD equivalent in these assets over the last fifty years, it should sell these assets either to a private enterprise willing to pay cash or sell the company to individual shareholders in the open stock market.

Over the last twenty years, India has lived the power of capitalistic markets in a number of industries. As a first step to raise the required capital, India must let these companies be owned, run, and managed, by private industry, where professional managers are responsible to answer to their shareholders. These managers will turn these companies into profitable ventures. This will then allow the government to generate tax revenues by taxing those profits, and taxing employees hired by these businesses. Using the proceeds from sales of these businesses and additional tax revenues, the Indian government can then focus on building infrastructure, protecting the environment, building strong defenses to protect its borders, provide law and order, and act as a referee for businesses to thrive.

Chapter 5

National Divestiture Policy

Since 1992, every elected Indian government has promised to divest government's ownership stake in the hundreds of companies run by the government. However, only a very few have been privatized. Even in instances where the government has sold its ownership in a company, it has been purchased by another government entity, mostly as no private institution or individuals will buy shares in a money-losing company run by government bureaucrats. Selling 5% of Steel Authority of India Limited, State Bank of India, or Oil and Natural Gas Corporation, has no real meaning. Such a sale will not change anything from an investor perspective. Until government is there to bail out these companies, management has no incentive to implement anything new or change the status quo, and employees have no motivation to do anything different.

Employees in all government-run companies are further organized through unions. It makes the situation strange, as on one hand government is the only shareholder and manager of the company, and at the same time it is also the entity responsible to protect the rights of its employees. Both roles represent two opposite sides. In most cases, government ends up as a protector of the employees' rights, and in the process ends up hurting its citizens who are the real shareholders of those companies represented by the government.

As an example, when the government recently decided to sell a small ownership in Coal India to private investors, Coal India employees went on strike. The government was forced to agree to the employees' demands with the full knowledge that a coal miner strike would stop power production all across the country and bring the country to its knees within weeks. Similar threats of strikes followed when government tried to discuss privatization of the national banks. In the end, government was forced to give bank employees a hike in their salaries and approve additional monthly leave for all government-run bank employees.

Unless government removes itself from all businesses as shareholder, India will never become a first-world economy. With the exception of China, where government rules with an iron fist, most successful world economies are run by private enterprises regulated by the laws of a democratic government. In these economies, government functions as either a regulator or referee to ensure their employees' rights are upheld in safe working environments under fair business practices.

Divestiture of stock of any of government-run companies has two major problems that must be addressed before the government can even discuss such sale of ownership of any of its companies to either a private entity or in the open stock market. First, there will be very few buyers willing to pay any higher than their asset value. Secondly, since the unions are deeply entrenched in these companies, it will be impossible for the new management to change the culture to one of performance unless they have the controlling interest in the company.

Today, government ownership and management of hundreds of the largest companies in every major industry is the heart of India's economic problems. To resolve this issue, government must publish a national divestiture policy. Government should publish a list of companies, along with a divestiture time line for each company (based on capital requirements), to be sold over a five-year-period. A national divestiture policy should list the following guidelines:

1. **Government will divest 20% of its ownership each year and will have divested all of its shares of the company within five years.**

This will allow stock markets not to overreact in case the company's stock trades on one of the public stock markets. It will also give management and employees a very firm notice that going forward the company has to generate enough revenue to pay or reduce costs for its day-to-day operations, and the company must transition to a performance-based culture.

2. **All new investors will have voting shares, and the government will convert its equity to non-voting shares.**

This will remove government from all day-to-day management and decision-making from the company. These companies have lost billions of taxpayers' money under government bureaucrats. It is time that a new approach is taken and the reins of these companies are handed over to the proven business professionals.

3. **Government should hand over company operations to an independent board for each company with a term of three years, approved by a majority of the private investors after the divestiture.**

As non-voting owners, government will not be making any management decisions, including the appointment of the management itself. Setting up an independent board approved by the new investors will force the company to think and act like a for-profit corporation. If needed, this will allow the new board members to replace bureaucrats running the companies with professional management. Management can then develop plans to restructure the company to build and grow the company's value for its shareholders. Initially, the term of this board should be for three years. After that, the shareholders (except the government) should choose the board annually.

4. **In the case of company termination of any employee within the first two years of divestiture, government will maintain their salary and benefits for the next twenty-four months. All employees within five years of retirement should be offered voluntary retirement.**

New management will need help to fix losses, management practices, morale, and a fifty-year-old work culture as a company transitions from a government job to for-profit shareholder control. As soon as government publicizes a divestiture policy, most unions and employees will force strikes to protect their future. Without any financial guarantees for a smooth transition, such strikes will not only create chaos, they will effectively shut down the country. So it is very important that the plan provides financial support and other ways to help individuals who the new management may not continue to keep on its payroll. A twenty-four-month severance will allow workers to be able to transition into a new position either in the same industry or in a new industry. Such severance will only be allowed for any terminations within the first two years of the divestiture. By offering early retirements, companies will be able to keep more of the younger workers in their jobs.

5. Government will assist in retraining the employee in the field of the employees' choice during the first two years after the divestiture.

In the same spirit, to help the laid-off employees, these employees should receive training to get a new job within the same company or start a new career in case the company is not able to keep them in another position. This will further help the transition, as well as impact the economy as a whole. Such training should be funded for any employee let go from the company for the first two years of the divestiture. After the two-year mark, government should enact a universal policy for companies to pay a certain amount towards the training for a new position.

6. Unions will not be permitted to strike within the first twenty-four months after a company's divestiture.

In exchange for early retirement, and a twenty-four-month severance and training for a new job, unions should be barred from striking during the two-year transition. This will not only help companies to get on their feet, it will help employees, and as well help the overall economy to grow without a temporary dip.

Overall, such a divestiture policy will enable companies to eschew seniority and instead hire the most qualified management. Companies will be able to incentivize improvement in their best employees and motivate their workforce to make the company profitable while removing the drag of non-performing employees. Such a policy will also open up possibilities for terminated employees, retraining them and assisting them in finding a job in another industry, once again becoming a productive member of the society.

Lastly, outlawing strikes in the twenty-four months following divestment will allow the new management to fix major issues in the organization and make the company competitive in the marketplace.

Chapter 6

Employment: India Urgently Needs Jobs, Jobs and More Jobs

The widely accepted measures of any economy's success are the size of its Gross Domestic Product and the employment it creates. Successful economic policies foster an environment of innovation, fair competition, make it easy to start a business, and create business-friendly tax policies, all resulting in employment for their citizens. These economic policies bolster employment and national wealth, in addition to bringing international recognition.

India has come a long way from the early 1990s, when government was the country's largest and only real employer. Today, India has privatized a number of industries, including banking, aviation, media and television, telecommunications, automobiles, medicine, and education, among others. The successful privatization of these industries has resulted in unprecedented employment growth and increase in India's overall GDP. Companies in these industries have created millions of white and blue-collar jobs. It has further created jobs in downstream services industries such as cooks, hairdressers, maids, laundresses, carpenters, welders, and many blue-collar jobs. India must privatize other industries such as power generation and distribution; all public transport, including railways and inter and intra state bus services; oil and gas production and distribution; management of all historic monuments; and every industry where private enterprise can manage these businesses more efficiently.

Today, India has the largest youth population in the world. More than 50% of India's population is below the age of twenty-five and 65% of the population is below the age of thirty-five. Even though privatization has created millions of jobs, India still has significant unemployment, as much as 30% among its youth. Every month, over 1-2 million new job seekers are entering the job market in India. As per independent reporting, India generated a total of 115,000 new jobs in 2015. This is not enough, and is a recipe for trouble down the road.

Unemployed youth can create unrest, and can be forced into crime for survival.

There are no simple shortcuts to creating jobs. India must adopt the three-step program to create jobs before it is too late.

1. **Privatize government-run industry and use the money in building public infrastructure, schools, law and order, legal infrastructure, and urgently needed local defense capability.**

Just by getting government out of all the large industries it runs could generate enough money to build tens of thousands of kilometers of roads, highways, and bridges. Such infrastructure construction will create hundreds of thousands of jobs overnight.

Similarly, money generated from selling government-run companies can be used to build or upgrade technology-enabled schools and additional infrastructure such as gyms and swimming pools and other basic amenities expected in twenty-first century school infrastructure; as well as hire and train of teachers; and train skills to college graduates that they lack.

India desperately needs to upgrade its law and order infrastructure such as buildings, technology and personnel. India needs to hire thousands of judges and police officers to not only manage crime, but to resolve millions of pending legal cases today.

Money can also be used to upgrade India's defense capabilities. It could be done by contracting to private companies to build next-generation fighter and transport planes, ships, tanks, missile systems, radars, submarines, and other military spending India plans to do over the next ten to twenty years. This will create hundreds of thousands of new jobs versus India paying foreign countries and helping those countries to boost their own employment. Most engineering graduates produced by India over the last fifty years are now employed by companies in the US and Europe building these technologies to be sold in countries like India.

Finally, money could also be used to clean up polluted rivers and the air, resulting in thousands of jobs in those fields.

2. Bring private enterprise to create jobs in new industries as well as old non-performing industries.

India should also open up sectors where it provides services to its citizens. For example, India should ask private companies to enter renewable energy markets to provide 100% of its electricity needs in the next twenty years by renewable energy options, such as solar, wind, and other renewable sources. It will reduce pollution dramatically and solve the energy crisis India has been unable to solve in the last seventy years.

Another industry that should be given to private companies to be funded by consumers is garbage collection and recycling. India should set a target of five years to recycle one hundred percent of its trash. Like Japan, Taiwan, and a number of other countries, India must plan to become a net zero trash producer. Given its population and limited land and trash pile-up, it creates a hazard of disease, which could create an epidemic anytime and cripple its economy.

A number of countries have passed laws that force manufacturers to create 100% recyclable packaging. Countries like Japan have now reached zero percent net trash. Japanese laws mandate manufacturers make all their packaging recyclable, enforce rules for its citizens to separate trash in various recyclable bins, and require trash collectors to recycle all trash. A similar infrastructure must be created at a national and state level at a war footing level in India. This will not only create thousands of jobs across various industries, it will also reduce pollution and eliminate infections and illnesses India's citizens get from piled-up trash in every street corner across the country.

In India today, all intercity rail and bus transport is managed by state or national government. There is almost no intra-city transport network except metro networks in a few large cities. Not only is intercity transport poorly funded, it is extremely unreliable and extremely uncomfortable for its users. Today, the aviation industry, which was opened to private industry just ten years ago, now competes successfully with India's subsidized railway services. A number of airlines are profitable whereas Indian Railways, Air India, and Indian Airlines lose massive amount of taxpayers' money annually. Once such industries are handed over with government oversight to private companies, intercity bus and railway transport will surely improve in quality. Given India's billion-plus population, such services will become extremely profitable segments of the transport industry. The same should be done for intra-city transport to replace the explosion of local cars in smaller and big cities. Auto-rickshaws, taxis, trams and other solutions used around the world must be selected and implemented by private industry based on a city's population, under government oversight. Private company ownership, and operations of both inter and intra-city transport will not only make services cheaper at improved quality, it will also create hundreds of thousands of new jobs across all Indian cities.

All these industries are also prime candidates for foreign direct investment. But such foreign investment must be considered with its pros and cons before investments are allowed. In the long run, FDI strategy could have dangerous consequences. Assuming India is able to attract large FDI to build infrastructure, how does the foreign investor recoup their money? For example, if Chinese companies plan to invest 100 billion USD equivalent to upgrade Indian railways, there should be a clear plan to pay the money back to Chinese companies, because if the Chinese companies are not able to recoup their money, they will abandon the project and it will be difficult to find other investors to fund similar projects across other industries. Similarly, types of FDI must be considered before getting into such arrangements. For example, a 100 billion USD loan can put a large burden on India's future generations. In the 1990s, Indonesia's large loans borrowed from the World Bank nearly brought the country to its knees, as they were unable to pay the loans back.

3. Let private industry innovate and create new markets.

In the US, every ten years a new industry is created by entrepreneurs, creating hundreds of thousands of new jobs and growing its economy exponentially. During the Second World War, the US economy grew dramatically with the manufacture of planes, tanks, submarines, and other equipment deployed in the war. After the war, US government invested heavily in building 41,000-mile long highways, bridges, and other infrastructure, creating hundreds of thousands of new jobs. In the 1960s, the US government and private industry partnership invented mainframe computers, creating tens of thousands of new jobs and growing the economy significantly. The 1970s and '80s saw innovation in semiconductors and personal computers, again growing the US economy dramatically. The 1990s and 2000s saw an explosion of Internet technologies, cell phones, and other related technologies, further growing the economy and creating millions of new jobs in the process. Today, US companies are inventing renewable energy sources, much faster ways to travel across the planet, as well as space travel, electric and hydrogen powered cars—there is no limit to where such inventions will take the economy but it will surely create millions of new jobs in the process.

It is possible for the US to create such large new employment because the US has created a system that makes it very simple for individuals with ideas to create a business, secure funding in a reasonable time frame, and bring the product to the open market without any need for dramatic approvals and regulations. With the right political will, a similar system can be replicated in India. India has the framework of democratic government, capitalistic markets, a willing and enterprising youth population, and ambition, to compete and make India one of the largest economies in the world. In the last thirty years, Indian engineers trained by India in its government-funded colleges have introduced a large number of innovations in the US market. Such companies have created hundreds of billions of dollars in the US GDP. There is no reason, given the right policies, that such innovation and value could not be created in India.

Chapter 7

Unleash India's Industry to Reduce Poverty

a. Infrastructure Development.

For any country to be a major economy in the twenty-first century, top-notch infrastructure is a basic requirement. If India aims to reach its full potential, it must invest substantially in basic road infrastructure in its small, medium, and large cities; coast-to-coast state and national highways; 24x7 power infrastructure; bus terminals and railway stations in all tier 1, 2, and 3 cities; best-of-class school infrastructure, large network of irrigation canals; state-of-the-art intra-city transit systems; world-class airports; and technologically equipped ports.

Developing just the transport infrastructure will require an investment of 1 trillion USD equivalent as estimated by established research groups. However, the specifics of the new infrastructure development must be considered carefully. Simply copying a Western model, which would introduce tens of thousands of miles of multi-lane highway, may not be the development that rural India needs. India must be mindful as to the efficacy and appropriateness of the proposed infrastructure before it is developed. Certainly, India should not follow a developed country's model that would call for transporting 1 billion people by cars. Rather, India would be better served by investing in mass transit systems, including subways, metro, buses, trams, and other mass transportation systems with best-in-class service with an aim of making transport within and between cities and states more efficient and comfortable.

For example, it would be preferable to build a bus lane or local train or tram on every four-lane highway than building eight-lane interstate highways. Similarly, within the city, a bike lane and a mechanism for smooth travel for two-wheelers should be considered as bicycles and two-wheelers constitute a major part of day-to-day traffic in smaller cities. Wherever possible, such infrastructure should be built with cash-neutral investments—i.e. it must be paid back by tolls and fees paid by customers wherever it possible. A 100-km four-lane

61

highway may cost up to 100 Million USD equivalent. If planned smartly, if 100,000 people use the highway every day, such an investment can by be paid by an average of Rupees 25 toll charge per vehicle in five years.

Government planners have to be smart to first build such highways in the most trafficked areas. India is not the first country to build highways and fund them without breaking the bank. Over a hundred small and large countries around the world have four to eight lane highways connecting all cities and towns. Most of these countries were able to make such an achievement in the twentieth century itself. Gasoline taxes, existing taxes and new taxes, and debt and private financing, should be used to build highways and other local infrastructure. Government should choose the right tools to fund individual projects.

India should incentivize private companies to invest in next-generation technologies such as battery or electric power, or ethanol or hydrogen-powered buses, or electric trains to run intra-city transport. Government should own the basic infrastructure and allow multiple private companies to run the transport vehicles by paying a fee to the government for using its lanes or tracks. This will not only reduce pollution, but also save a lot of foreign exchange India spends in importing gasoline from the international markets.

Today, there is big push to invest up to 100 billion USD equivalent of taxpayers' money in India's airport infrastructure. India should focus on quality and not quantity for air travel infrastructure development. After twenty-five years of deregulation of India's air travel, less than 5% of its people have ever traveled in an airplane. It may take another fifteen years for that number to double. Given the majority of India's population drives two-wheelers and bicycles, India's immediate focus should be on investing in roads, highways, and intra-city infrastructure. For air travel, India should first limit its development in the largest twenty-five cities. The next twenty city airports should be given taxpayers' money only if air travel shows much more dramatic growth.

For India to compete with large economies around the world, public and private investment must be made in large ports to keep up with the growth of international trade. Given that creating a new port or even expanding an existing port facility is highly expensive, India should allow domestic and international private investors to fund such a capacity increase. As a port business can easily show a return on investment, it will be easy for domestic and international port operators to bid, build, and manage port terminals with private investments.

The Indian government owns twelve ports around the country. In 2017, government budgeted 124 billion USD equivalent to upgrade and expand existing ports. India should not only let the private investors make this investment but also sell its existing investment in Indian ports to the highest bidder and use this money in other infrastructure investments, such as schools much needed for India's youth.

India should adopt the model of primary and secondary school infrastructure funding used in the US and other Western countries. The number of primary and secondary schools in a city should be established based on a city's population. For example, there should be a primary school (grade K-5) for every 500-1,000 students and a middle school (6-8) for every three primary schools and an intermediate college (9-12) for every five middle schools. Students must be mandated to attend a particular school based on their address, thereby reducing commute times and absenteeism. Schools should receive the required investment based on level of schooling, number of students, and their curriculum requirements.

Today, India lacks basic facilities such as toilets in all of its schools. It is very basic for schools in most developed countries to have a classroom equipped with multiple blackboards and whiteboards; overhead projectors; Internet-enabled tablet devices and other teaching aids based on the class level; and sports infrastructure such as basic playgrounds at all school levels. Additionally, all school buildings should be equipped with science and computer labs and air conditioning, as India's weather remains intolerably hot throughout the school year. In the twenty-first century, a school cannot be in the business of education without an uninterrupted power source. All schools must be powered by a local solar power source providing 24/7 uninterrupted power.

Middle schools must be equipped with sports infrastructure, such as running tracks, gyms, soccer fields, badminton, basketball, volleyball and tennis courts, for students to get involved in these sports at an early age. Large-investment facilities such as swimming pools and sports stadiums should be built at the intermediate college levels.

Today, children in developed countries like the US have 100% accessibility to the Internet with mobile devices provided by the schools. Children from every income level everywhere are able to learn about any subject as early as primary school. This helps them not only become much more aware but also helps them learn about their own interests and talents early. This provides them time to pursue fields of their choice, produces diverse talents in various professions, and leaders in all professions. Such a philosophy has allowed students in the US to excel in every field including music, cinema, writing, engineering, medicine, arts, basic sciences, mathematics, finance, teaching and various sports.

Currently hundreds of millions of people in India do not have access to running drinking water. Major cities have days of water blackouts. Investments must be made to make basic necessities like drinking water available to every citizen. Connecting rivers whenever sensible, storing water during the times of monsoon, desalinization, stopping wells from deteriorating water tables, and other avenues of providing water should be explored.

Over 50% of India's population lives on agriculture today. Required investments must be made in providing water for irrigation to all of India's agricultural land. With climate change impacting rain patterns and melting of glaciers over the last fifty years, India must look into all possible solutions for needs of the farmers, because with India's population expected to reach 1.5 billion by 2050, shortages of water for irrigation will turn into shortages of food for millions.

Over the last fifty years, with its dramatic population surge, India now has over forty-seven cities with over 1 million people in population. Major cities have become mega-cities. But at the same time, there has been no investment made in their most basic infrastructure such as sewer systems. A large number of cities next to a river dump raw sewage in the rivers. Sewer systems in the 500 largest cities must be upgraded under the first national infrastructure plan.

Another area of investment that must be considered is public housing to eliminate homelessness and slums across all major cities. Today, hundreds of thousands of children and poor families live on footpaths, under bridges, and highways in India. In public-private partnerships, investments must be made in low cost public housing to move people out of the slums and streets, because unless a solution is found for such homelessness and slums, children growing up under such conditions have no future. Without a livelihood, these children will be forced into crime. Government must find way to finance building low cost housing to accommodate homeless people, as well as find a way to re-settle people currently living in unauthorized slums.

Such investment, if planned correctly, will produce millions of new jobs in the infrastructure sector. It will grow India's GDP significantly as such infrastructure will make the day-to-day functioning of most businesses more efficient, which in turn will require more workers to be employed in the overall economy.

b. Living without Electricity - A Very Basic Utility in First World Economies. We Deserve Better!

Today, 25% percent of India's population, over 250 million people, does not have access to electricity. Across India, people live though summer temperatures above 45 degrees Celsius in major cities and winter lows of -10 to 0 degrees Celsius across northern India, all without dependable electricity. Only fifty kilometers outside major cities, daily power cuts for more than five hours are common. The generations that have grown up in these unfortunate conditions are resigned to such difficulties. India's politicians and policy makers in every government make promises for improvement, but year-over-year the situation gets worse and life goes on. Personally, this was the hardest part of being a child growing up in India, living in places where summer temperatures extended for nine months of the year and one had to live without fans or lights for twelve hours a day. India's average individual with access to electricity consumes one-fifteenth electricity of the average consumer in a developed country, and one fourth that of its neighbor China. The people of India deserve better.

India holds the largest deposits of coal in the world, but it is not able to produce enough coal to provide electricity to its entire people. The majority of India's power is generated by government-controlled organizations that mine coal, government-controlled transportation organizations such as railways that ship coal to government-controlled power generation plants that distribute electricity through the government-owned power grid. Rampant corruption, pilferage, the sale of stolen coal in the black market, extremely inefficient delivery of coal to power plants, and theft of electricity by unauthorized connections by consumers, are reported widely. Since highly inefficient unionized government employees run the whole supply chain, no one can be held responsible for providing poor service or terminated for the ultimate situation.

The whole power infrastructure, starting from the mining of the coal, its transportation to power plants, and electrical production and distribution must be privatized. Government should lease all mines to private companies to mine coal. That would automatically remove any chances of stealing, as the leasing company would implement safeguards to protect it from theft. Similarly, all transport of coal should be privatized, with private companies running its own trains or trucks. Today, railway subsidies to transport coal not only make railways lose money, it creates possibilities of corruption and theft as the coal is transported from mines to the plants over thousands of miles across multiple states.

Once the three entities are privatized, they will enforce accountability to protect their own profitability and survival. Additionally, once these companies are in the private sector, shareholders will hire skilled management capable of making these companies efficient and profitable. Electricity prices must be regulated to ensure that these companies cannot charge arbitrary prices to their customers. Most successful world economies have the private sector mine the coal and other resources to produce and distribute electricity to consumers now well for over fifty years. These governments keep oversight so that power companies do not overcharge their customers. The government approves all rate increases to keep up with inflation and other issues at all steps in the generation and distribution process. These countries not only provide 24/7 electricity to their populations, they also have surplus power as the demand for electricity grows with increased business and population.

India must invest in alternative energy technologies with the knowledge that India's billion-plus population will eventually consume all of its coal currently being used to produce electricity. At the same time, India will also pay a huge environmental cost in burning coal. Out of all available technologies, India must choose to invest in solar power first. India has an abundance of sun-covered areas all year round. Over the last few years, India's policy makers have opened the industry to private companies that are moving towards creating large solar farms. It is only part of the solution, however, as solar farms do not produce any electricity in the night.

Most countries around the world diversifying into solar power are working differently. These countries are encouraging investments by homeowners and other real estate owners to generate electricity from their homes and buildings for their individual consumption and sell the excess electricity back to the power company. Such a plan across the country must be developed to reduce India's dependence on coal or oil-based electricity production. Every building owner must be mandated to install or lease solar power generation equipment to first use for its own requirement and sell any access electricity to the city grid. As electric storage technology matures, homes and buildings can then also store electricity locally to power lights and other needs during the night hours. Such a system can help solve India's power problems over the next decade.

Other alternate sources of power generation like hydro, wind, and other renewable energy solutions must be allowed to enter the market. India being a vast country with a rich geographical diversity allows for the use of different natural resources. India has already made large investments in hydroelectric power, and wherever economical, further investments must be made. Brazil and China currently produce four and eight times more hydroelectric power than India. If China and Brazil could create such capability in the last thirty years, India should have done the same. India must invest wisely in hydroelectric power to supplement power requirements in certain parts of the country where India's geography allows it to create dams. Such dams could also help in storing water to help avoid devastating floods in the monsoon season.

Although tempting, India must avoid generating nuclear power. Nuclear power is accident-prone, and a small mistake or natural disaster like in Japan and Russia could wipe out densely populated Indian cities. Additionally, the storage of nuclear waste is a major concern, as no country has been able to solve problem of storing it. Leakages into soil and water have led to disease outbreaks such as cancer in cities around the world. India should wait to use nuclear power for power generation, until a nuclear reactor technology becomes available, which allows recycling of nuclear waste.

Lastly, the power distribution network should be privatized to enable power distribution companies to charge consumers directly. According to a 2014 World Bank report, power theft and inefficiency of the power distribution organization is a major contributor for lack of electricity to over 300 million people across India. In 2011, with lack of collections, and electricity theft, power distribution companies took debts of over 77 billion USD equivalent. This is after government paid 5.5 billion USD equivalent to pay off the debts of electricity companies in 2001. If these companies are run efficiently and profitably—i.e. so that there is no theft and electricity is sold at the price per unit based on cost of efficient production and money was collected properly from all of its users—government could have saved this money. It could have been used to set up 15,000 new hospitals and 123,000 schools, which are needed urgently. There are more and more reasons for government to get out from all aspects of production and distribution of electricity in India and let the private sector run these companies as done all across the world.

c. Water – It's a Basic Human Right and a National Emergency!

As a kid growing up in the Himalayan foothills and mountain towns, water was omnipresent. I lived in a city where the largest rivers met and ultimately became the Ganges. By my early teens, I was lucky to visit the places from where the Ganges and Yamuna began. It was amazing and overwhelming to see nature's immensity and magic. Large rivers, snow-capped mountains, lakes, and running water in the cities I lived in were commonplace.

It was incredible to see how in the next twenty years the whole water landscape changed. I saw streams stopped flowing in the Himalayan foothills. Cities, which had 24/7-running water, started to limit running water for part of the day. Places, which saw a regular and long monsoon season started to get limited rain. According to the World Health Organization, today, over 100 million Indian citizens do not have access to clean water at all. Availability of running water has become a serious concern all across India, from the Himalayan foothills to the downstream cities, up to India's coasts.

Seventy years after Independence from British, India is unable to provide easy access to drinking water to 36 percent of its population. No large Indian city is able to provide 24/7-running water to its residents. Such dramatic shortage of running water from rivers has forced pumping of groundwater by farmers. With free electricity given by the government to farmers, and India's laws allowing landowners to own their ground water, millions of private wells have been dug to pump water all across the country. Usage of India's underground water is now more than that of the US and China combined. India is currently using 250 cubic kilometers of underground water, which is equivalent to a quarter of total underground water used across the world.

Water tables in Indian cities have dropped hundreds of feet, threatening availability of groundwater even for drinking purposes. Lack of underground water for irrigation in the next decade will create havoc for India's section of population that depends on irrigation. Such an impact is already evident is the states of Andhra Pradesh, Gujarat, Maharashtra, Karnataka, and Tamil Nadu, where farmers are protesting and committing suicide in large numbers. Just in the state of Maharashtra, 23,000 farmers committed suicide from 2009-2016. Even though 18,241 farmers committed suicide in 2004, successive governments have failed to find an immediate solution to the problem. Since 2013, over 12,000 farmer suicides have been reported every year. According to a number of studies done by various organizations; India's water consumption per year will double by 2050.

India is planning to connect all rivers to make sure that the water is distributed across the country in the months of less rainfall in certain regions. The Indian government has recently started work on this, and it is estimated to cost 168 billion USD equivalent to connect thirty-seven Himalayan and peninsular rivers through thirty canals and 3,000 reservoirs. The plan calls for canals from 50-100 meters wide, and over 150,000 kilometers in length once all the canals are constructed. A number of ecologists have raised serious concerns about the project in the long run. It is an expensive solution and may not work as planned due to climate change. Indian rivers are unable to provide water in its current path because of overuse of water, as well as less snow in the Himalayan glaciers year over year. At the same time, states are blocking water downstream as they are stretched thin for water to be used locally.

To provide enough drinking water to India's growing population, India must enforce laws against unlimited usage of underground water. At the same time, India must invest heavily in storing its rainwater during the monsoons. There is no infrastructure to store rainwater, while the majority of the country depends on rainwater for irrigation and other water needs. India currently stores only 6% of its rainwater versus 250% by developed countries. Historically, each Indian village had a pond to store water, which they could use for various purposes. Most palaces and forts stored water from rainfall in large quantities to use it all year long. As city sprawl consumed villages, such ponds disappeared, and overall water storage completely stopped. Given India's population depends on rainfall for irrigation and drinking water, massive investment is needed in rainwater storage and recycling of water in large and second tier cities with populations over 250,000. With forecasts of melting of Himalayan glaciers and irregular rainfalls due to global warming, rainwater storage is the most effective way to fight water shortages.

A public-private partnership should be created to build rainfall storage infrastructure in every village, town, and city. Wherever possible, government land should be leased to private companies to create storage pools or underground storage to store rainwater. This water can be used in times of shortages. Prices should be regulated by a government agency to make sure private companies do not overcharge for the water like it is done in the most Western countries. All such water storage, sewage, and cleaning up of rivers will require significant investment, and must be funded through fees, taxes, and private investment. This will require billions of USD equivalent in investment, creating millions of new jobs and adding billions in India's GDP.

d. Environment: Fix it or Live a Painful Life Sentence.

India needs to invest urgently in restoring its environment for its future generations. Pollution has invaded every aspect of people's day-to-day lives. In the last fifty years, India has cut down millions of trees, polluted most of its rivers through sewage and industrial pollutants, introduced millions of tons of pollutants into the air, and left filth everywhere, to the point that the country resembles a trash dumping ground.

India's largest cities are the most polluted cities in the world. The air is polluted by automobiles, industrial and power plant exhaust; rivers are polluted by industrial and human waste; ground water is polluted by chemicals used in fertilizers; and large sections of cities are polluted by human waste piling up on every street corner. A large percentage of children growing up in Indian cities are afflicted with weak lungs, asthma, and other respiratory afflictions and numerous other viruses. In November 2015, India's leading newspapers reported that Delhi's particulate matter (particles smaller than 2.5 microns and 10 micron in diameter) reached up to twenty times the acceptable safe limit.

Crop burning is one of the other main sources of the annual air pollution that occurs in the fall and early winter. Public reports reveal that over 500 million tons of crop waste is burnt every year, releasing pollutants that continue to sully the air throughout the winter months. Crop burning must be stopped. Any violators must be fined and jailed as criminals. At the same time, safe disposal alternatives must be provided to dispose of agricultural waste.

Major investment is needed in moving power production away from coal and gasoline-fired power plants. Power generation should be replaced by bringing private enterprises to first treat exhaust to reduce pollution and to install renewable energy sources over time. India should roll out a year-over-year target for the next twenty years to bring air pollution across the country down to non-hazardous levels.

In 2015, India produced 2.274 Giga-tons of carbon dioxide, making India the world's third-largest emitter of carbon dioxide after the United States at 5.414 Giga-tons, and China at 10.357 Giga-tons.

Even though India produced much less per capita carbon dioxide pollution, it is still in India's interest to reduce carbon dioxide pollution wherever it can for its own good.

In conjunction with investing in public transportation, India must limit the number of cars allowed in its urban centers. Most international metropolitan cities limit the number of cars allowed in the city during the office hours. India should implement strict regulations on all cars' and trucks' fuel efficiency, and pollution standards. As discussed earlier in the book, investment must be made in electric, battery, and solar-powered public-transport infrastructure, and India should look to take a lead in investing in the latest emerging technologies such as hydrogen-powered automobile infrastructure.

From rural India to the India's large urban centers, one can smell the stench of stagnant water and blocked streams for miles. It is amazing that millions of people live in these areas and commute by it without raising concerns with their city, state, or national governments. India's largest sewer systems have not been upgraded since they were built fifty years ago. As a result, blocked rainwater mixes with domestic wastewater, clogging up streets and increasing filth and disease everywhere. Standing filthy water has become a part of normal life in India. The average citizen has become resigned to it and no longer considers it pollution. Waterborne diseases are becoming commonplace, which has marked higher fatal incidences of kidney stones, diarrhea, dengue fever, and malaria. One-fifth of all communicable diseases in India are now related to unsafe water. INCLEN reports that water pollution kills more than 580 people in India every day.

According to the 2011 World Health Organization report, only 166 cities out of over 8,000 treat sewage partially, and only eight cities treat sewage completely. At least ten cities dump sewage directly into the Ganges. This results in the dumping of approximately 30 billion liters of untreated sewage in India's rivers. A hundred cities dump its raw sewage directly into the Ganges alone. Over 400 million people living next to rivers use river water for drinking. Millions more bathe in the Ganges every year due to its mythological status. The impact of such water contamination is astounding. Diarrhea from waterborne diseases alone kills over 200,000 children under the age of five every year. Millions of children develop enteropathy due to exposure of fecal bacteria in the water, resulting in the stunting in millions of children. This number has grown significantly over the last five years. This can only be stopped by major investment in building toilets in every household and sewage plants in each city.

On the industrial side, chemical manufacturing, sugar production, distilleries, pulp and paper, textile, mining, and fertilizer plants and tanneries are the leading industries dumping their waste into India's rivers and other water supplies—releasing toxic metals such as arsenic, chromium, and lead. India must enforce its laws urgently to stop these offenders, and impose severe penalties to all companies guilty of such pollution.

Government should not only pass but enforce laws and charge severe penalties for all river pollution to stop immediately, and must invest significantly for rivers to again become free of chemicals and other pollutants. Such an investment must come from penalties or the volunteering of funds from the industries responsible for polluting India's rivers over the years. Additionally, a temporary tax should be charged on certain industrial sectors to create an emergency fund until a cleanup of rivers is completed.

Indian cities generate over 200 million tons of solid waste annually. India today looks like a trashcan, with every city street corner and village filled with trash and filth. India has created a massive consumption economy over the last twenty years. But the government policy has failed to tackle the increasing amount of waste. A call for private investment in creating a recycling ecosystem to collect, process, and recycle, as done by the most developing countries around the world, must be developed. Countries like Japan have eliminated trash completely by passing and enforcing laws to recycle one hundred percent of the trash generated in the country. All manufacturers are required to use 100% recyclable packaging, all citizens are required to separate trash in various recyclable bins, and trash processing companies are required to recycle 100% of the trash generated in the country. India must implement new laws to restrict pollution and implement solutions used around the world to tackle all pollution in day-to-day life, as it is our responsibility to the future generations of India to leave its environment better than the one they inherited.

India's municipalities have failed spectacularly over the last fifty years in managing city infrastructure, keeping cities clean from garbage, and keeping up city sewage and drainage systems. Mayors must be charged to contract all city services to private companies. Municipalities should be held responsible by their citizens to keep the cities clean, safe, and provide key basic services.

At the rate India's population is migrating to cities, increases in the pollution of air, water, and trash will continue to increase. The issue of pollution is not unique to India or Indian cities. Most European countries and the US have dealt with air pollution successfully as their economies became dependent on industrial production. In the US, New York in 1970s and Los Angeles in 1990s can be a guide to solve such pollution issues, as both cities were able to reduce industrial and automobile pollution significantly. For most of the world, these are twentieth century problems. Basic policy enforcement can solve air and water pollution in a decade's time.

The government must recognize environmental policy as a priority, and be aware that failure to enact changes will result in increased disease, reduced life expectancy, and a countrywide death sentence.

Fixing all the environmental issues is not only good for people, but it will also create hundreds of thousands of new jobs, and healthier people will be more productive, adding to the overall GDP of the country. Fixing environmental issues will also considerably reduce expenses of all medical treatments paid by India's taxpayers through its government-funded healthcare system.

e. Trash clean up in India: Can Not be Done by just Broom and Shovels.

India can create a huge new private industry in garbage collection and recycling trash. It will not only add significantly to India's GDP, but will also create hundreds of thousands of new jobs in every village, town, and city across the country.

It is incredible to see as how a country of over 1 billion people are not outraged or ask their local government, city administrators, state and national governments to keep their towns and cities clean. From the center of India's capital, New Delhi, to the major cities like Bangalore, to any small city from north to south and east to west, India is cluttered with trash. Bus and railway stations are always overflowing with trash. City markets, back streets, and even highways have trash everywhere. Open sewers spilling water on streets, stagnant water pools in the middle of main city roads, and streets littered with wrappers, paper, and rotten biomass are a common sight in India. Even the hill towns, once famous for their pristine beauty, are blanketed with trash and stagnant water pollution.

Trash and other solid waste pollution are already creating serious health hazards. India is wrecked by outbreaks of malaria, dengue fever, swine flu, encephalitis, and tuberculosis, killing tens of thousands of people every year. New waterborne diseases and drug resistant bugs are being identified. No one can say with certainty that these are a direct result of waste pollution; however, it is a foregone conclusion that if India fails to enact comprehensive waste management policies, severe disease outbreaks will spread more dramatically and may kill hundreds of thousands of people.

Despite the gravity of the situation, it seems that all of India's people and policymakers have just become used to it. Trash has a become part of everyday life. Most people, whether they are just passing by, or in some cases even living right next to piled-up trash, do not object to their living conditions. It is not uncommon to see up to a million people living next to a trash dump, or miles of standing, stinky water. Even though India's religious texts preach hygiene and cleanliness, India has allowed the situation to get to this extreme. Systematic spread of disease among children and elderly is ignored.

Every community park is a trash bin. It is not uncommon in buses or trains to see people to eat food and drop trash right on the floor or just throw it out of the window. It is not that such behavior is typical of India's uneducated masses. Even a large number college-educated folks, who want India to become the best country in the world, throw food wrappers out of their moving cars, or an earthen teacup out of a moving public train without any hesitation. These are the same folks who talk non-stop about the cleanliness of the last city they vacationed outside India and how everyone followed the traffic rules, but at the same time take no personal responsibility or leadership in raising the issue in their local community. The same folks would put all building construction materials right on the road, blocking all traffic for months, to build a house or a house extension. They would park their two cars on the narrow public street without worrying about inconvenience to their neighbors or to the local community.

One might point to India's high population density to justify this situation. However, most major international cities with high population densities keep their cities clean. These cities have built systems of severe fines for littering, set up trash collection bins in all locations, planned door-to-door trash pick-up at all public, street-corner, and business locations, and made large investments in recycling plants and trash dumps.

With the growth of the consumer economy in India in the last twenty-five years, the trash issue has become worse across the country. The present waste management system depends on local municipalities run by government employees to keep the cities clean. Similar to all government jobs, they lack both motivation and fear of consequences, even if filth and trash pile up everywhere. If trash pickup and the recycling industry were to be privatized, and the same contract awarded to a private company, India would look like a Western country overnight. It is again an issue of failure of policy-making by local, state, and national governments.

India is too large of a country to be cleaned by brooms and shovels. For India to clean up its streets, it must privatize trash collection, set and implement fines for littering or leaving trash in front of a house, develop and implement a national recycling policy, issue standards for landfills, including mandating plastic liners and groundwater leakage monitoring at all landfill sites, and allocate resources to the management of waste processing. In most developed countries, waste management is a multi-billion dollar industry. Private companies are contracted to collect, process, and recycle all trash. These companies have made billions of dollars of investments in modern equipment and manpower to fund the collection, processing, and recycling of trash.

Additionally, since keeping the city clean is a municipal function, municipalities should be allowed to raise local taxes and fees as needed. Municipalities should also be allowed to raise money through other sources such as bonds to build local infrastructure. Residents should be mandated to pay monthly fees to private companies to pick up, process, and recycle trash.

Today, countries like the US produce ten times more trash per person than India is producing currently. But India can expect per capita trash to continue to go up as the economy expands. With India's population being multiple times that of the US and one third of the landmass, a major framework to solve India's trash problem is urgently needed.

Trash and solid waste pollution hurts India in multiple ways. In addition to spreading disease and contaminating ground water, it also hurts India's tourism employment, and ultimately impacts India's GDP significantly. Europe and a number of other Asian cities attract far more tourists because of their cleanliness and superior transport infrastructure than India. Even though Indian cities have a lot more historical value and are much cheaper to visit, India ranks far below most European countries, and even smaller Asian countries, in terms of number of foreign tourists.

In the last fifty years, a unique culture of individualism has evolved in India. Individualism has taken precedence over the community's needs and safety. Whatever once belonged to the community has now been lost. The quality of all shared resources, including air, water, community parks, and roads, have deteriorated. If India plans to eradicate poverty and gain its place in the developed world, it must reverse this course. Community interests must be enforced above those of individuals. Local police departments must uphold laws and enforce stiff fines for misdemeanors, including parking and littering on public land, and littering in public parks and highways. It is interesting to note that Indian citizens who immigrate to developed countries follow the local rules and find a trash can to throw their trash into rather than littering on the road or a in a park. This is because most developed countries enforce their laws, and their citizens adhere to these regulations. It is not inherent culture that overlooks littering, it is the lack of enforcement that allows people to litter and get away with it.

f. Banking: Must sell Government Ownership in Public Sector Banks.

India's banking sector controls 63% of India's overall financial assets, valued at approximately 1.3 trillion USD equivalent. Between 2009 and 2013, India's CNX Nifty Banking Index rose by an annual rate of 14.05% vs. 12.05% growth in Nifty vs.11.00% growth in the S&P 500 Banking Index. Interestingly, India's private banks were responsible in generating most of this growth. The comparison between public and private banks between 2009 and 2013 reveals that the country's largest public bank, the State Bank of India, offered returns at the annual rate of 3.18%, while the two largest private banks, HDFC Bank and ICICI Bank, respectively returned 22.16% and 15.88% per year. By the end of 2014, public banks' gross nonperforming asset ratio was over 5%, while the private banks' gross nonperforming asset ratio was much lower at 2%.

Thanks to the liberalization of the banking industry in the 1990s, private banks are thriving. There are now equal numbers of public and private ATMs in Indian cities, and the overall service in private banks is more pleasant and customer friendly than the service provided by the public banks.

Since the government owns public banks, the government is always on the hook to pay for their annual losses accrued through bad loans, banks' inability to terminate poor-performing employees, and outdated hiring practices. Because of good customer service, a large number of retail and small business customers have moved from public banks to the private sector banks. Since the government does all its business through the public banks, the public bank employees have been able to keep the government hostage by threatening to strike for increased compensation in exchange for sub-standard work and the guarantee that the status quo will remain in full force. Since public bank employees cannot be terminated and continue to lose customers to private banks year over year, the public banks have become a drain on taxpayers.

One of the major issues of public banks in India is the large number of outstanding bad loans made by these banks. The key reason of the financial crisis in the world in 2008 was due to bad home loans made by bank employees to get higher bonuses, irrespective of the person who took the loan was unable to pay it back. With India's public bank bad debt equaling to ten percent of India's GDP, these bad loans have put India's economy to severe financial exposure. As of March 2017, public sector banks bad loans were equal to 75% of the total value of these banks.

As an overall policy solution, the Indian government must sell the private banks to either other private banks or sell government ownership of these banks in the open stock market. As per the industry experts, as part of transition of public banks from government ownership to non-government shareholders, the bad loans problem has to be fixed. Public banks currently have a large portfolio of land holdings as part of their assets. Today, the ten largest public banks hold over 10-15 billion USD equivalent of land holdings. As part of the transition, government should divest all of the land holdings in their portfolio to clean the banks' balance sheet, as well as pay for infrastructure and other financial needs India has today.

Similarly, public banks also have a large withholdings of approximately 10 billion USD equivalent in UTI Mutual Fund (owned by the government through State Bank of India, Life Insurance Corporation of India, Bank of Baroda, and Punjab National Bank). Government should also sell UTI withholdings to make up for the bad loans before private shareholders are allowed to purchase public banks assets.

Lastly, banks are also withholding all the personal properties of individuals who left for Pakistan as "Custodian of Enemy Property." Recently, in 2016, government passed a law to take over these properties. Government should sell these properties to further use the proceeds to clean up public banks' balance sheets, and use any additional money for infrastructure development.

Even though India passed a new bankruptcy law recently, banks collecting on these loans, or forcing the companies into bankruptcy to collect against these loans, is a long way away. Unfortunately, none of India's major problems can be resolved until India's legal system is reformed. As discussed earlier, Indian courts have millions of pending cases, with additional millions of new cases piling up year over year.

For India to succeed financially, the government must immediately privatize the public banks. It can be done either by selling the banks' shares to the individuals, or large non-government shareholders, or auctioning the public banks' assets to other private banks. Private banks could be allowed to put a bid for public bank branches in areas they currently have a weak presence. At the same time, private banks must guarantee to run bank branches in rural areas and places in with lower population for ten years after such auction. By selling its ownership in the public banks in the open marketplace, the government will achieve two goals simultaneously: one, reducing the funding requirements for public banks, and second, steadily raising funds for improved public infrastructure and other public reforms. Furthermore, as part of divestiture of public banks, government should transfer a portion of its business to the private sector banks and close branches in large cities where private banks have already grown and taken over large market share.

In a recent effort, India has been looking to move to a cashless economy to reduce corruption and bring transparency in financial transactions. Such efforts are in the right direction, but Indian elites must see things in perspective. In a country where 80% of the population lives on 2 USD equivalent per day, the idea that people have the means and ability to pay electronically and manage finances using some kind of online access to banking is utterly absurd. In a country where opening a bank account is a cumbersome process, it is really not practical to assume that India can become a cashless transaction country even in the next twenty-five years.

If the government fails to remove itself from the public banking business sector immediately, India's financial system will continue to damage the country's economy, hemorrhaging taxpayers' money while allowing unions and bank employees to hold it hostage. But if all such recommendations are implemented, India's private sector will become much more powerful in giving out large loans to fund infrastructure projects, as well as loans to businesses and individuals based on their creditworthiness, growing the economy tenfold. In turn, that will create millions of new jobs in every industry, and build a circle of growth.

g. **Indian Railways: Let's make it First World.**

After completing my high school education, I had the chance to spend a summer in Delhi. New Delhi's railway station was recently inaugurated and it was brand spanking new. All the platforms and the bridge connecting them were built with red bricks. A nice park was created at the entrance. It made me feel proud to see a structure befitting the central railway station of the capital of the country.

On the other hand, as I travelled back and forth between the US and India in the 1990s, I always found New Delhi International Airport to be exactly the opposite, a building non-befitting the international airport in the country's capital. This was the first impression of the country to an international visitor. I had once mentioned to a friend, as a joke, that even the New Delhi railway station looked better than its airport—and then I went back to the New Delhi railway station in early 2010. The bright red brick walkways were all eroded by a couple of inches by millions of people who had used the station over the last twenty years. Trash bins were overflowing, with flies all over the platforms. It was an incredibly hot day but a number of the fans were not working. The nice park at the entrance, which was once full of trees, had been covered with pavement. There were more people on the platform than the platform could really accommodate. A number of trains were running late. The inbound Delhi train, from which I had gone to pick up my friend, was running late by twelve hours from its scheduled arrival.

Rail transportation is the bloodline of Indian travel, with millions of people traveling daily around the country by train to visit family, move between cities, and even commute to work. Indian railways lose 5 billion USD equivalent annually, providing a sub-standard service to its customers. In its latest revised pay scale issued by the government, Indian Railways will pay an additional 5 billion USD equivalent in its payroll shortly as well, effectively losing over 8 billion USD equivalent every year.

With an average speed of 54 km/hour, it takes days for travelers to get across the country. Indian Railways has one of the poorest safety records. In the last six years, Indian railways have had over 800 accidents, killing and injuring hundreds of people. At best, India's train stations are dirty, and at worst they are outright filthy. Due to lack of any law enforcement, most passengers throw their trash on the train tracks or on the platform. In a large number of train stations, trash bins are usually overflowing due to lack of a waste management system. Most station platforms and trains are overcrowded. There is usually a higher chance that the train will be running late rather than on time. Travelers are resigned to delays of up to twenty-four hours. Travelers have to make reservations months in advance due to limited capacity on each route. It is a common sight to find local commuters overcrowding the reserved coaches between major cities on the longer routes. The general compartments, which are mostly used by the poorest people of India, are over-crowded and extremely uncomfortable to travel.

I had an unfortunate experience traveling in an Indian Railways general compartment on my way to collect my passport from the state passport office. My trip sums up an experience for an average poor Indian citizen travel on Indian Railways. I would not wish such an experience even on an enemy.

I had to take the train from a city just seventy kilometers outside of Delhi. Since it was summer, I decided to travel in the night to beat the heat. Even at 10 p.m., it was still 35 C with 100% humidity, and as one would expect in India, the station was without power. Sweating profusely due to the unbearable heat, being stung by mosquitoes in the darkness, and suffering the unbearable stench of overflowing trash around me, I found myself praying for the train to make it on time. Since I had to travel on a moment's notice, I did not have a reservation. I knew that the general coaches were in the back of the train. As the train pulled up on the station, I rushed with others to get on the train to find a seat in the first general compartment.

As I reached the first coach, it was way too overcrowded even to get in. I tried the next one and then the next one. Soon I realized that the fourth coach was the end of the train. It was that compartment or I waited until morning at the Pleasantville station behind me. I used all the strength I could gather and made my way onto the train. Not only was there not a single empty seat in the coach, every inch of space on the coach floor was occupied by people like a herd of cattle. I found enough space next to a stench-filled toilet for me to sit on my suitcase and wait to get to my destination.

It is painful for me to imagine that a majority of India's population travels in such conditions in the twenty-first century. It is inhuman. But, since only the very poor travel in the general compartments, very little attention has been given to these coaches over the last thirty-five years.

This state of affairs is not acceptable. The people of India deserve better. People deserve clean stations, faster trains running on time, and better facilities across all levels of rail travel. Why does India lack a comfortable and efficient rail system? Like other businesses, the Indian government believes it can run the transportation system better than private industry. Therein lies the problem. In a recent proposal, Indian Railways requested 500 billion USD equivalent to upgrade its rail infrastructure. It also proposed partnerships between private and public sectors in order to create an expanded fleet of faster trains. First, where will this money come from? Second, even if Indian Railways raises the money by taking on debt, like everything else, change is impossible as long as the Indian government continues to run the rail system through subsidies, and without any accountability. If India is committed to improving its rail transportation, the first priority must be to privatize the complete railways system. Indian Railways must sell every component, except the stations and rails, to private enterprise: the trains, the reservation system, and all hard assets must be sold off. Private enterprises have a better understanding of how to run operations better than any government. Multiple rail companies should be allowed to run trains on any route where trains are overcrowded and there are long reservation times. The funds raised from these asset sales should be invested in upgrading the railway stations and the national rail grid. At the same time, national standards for rail transportation must be established and enforced.

Once these changes are in effect, Indian Railways should then collect rent on the rails and stations from the private companies and put these funds towards expanding the rail network and creating new stations. However, it will be important that all upgrades, maintenance, and extensions of the rail network must be also contracted out to the private companies.

This model has worked very well in growing air travel in India. Whereas Air India continues to lose billions of USD equivalent every year, private airlines are operating profitably and growing year over year. Government owns the airports and charges airlines to use airport facilities. Airports are upgraded and managed by the private companies. Such a model has worked so well that airlines are now competing with Indian Railways on long routes, as for the same price travelers can travel in few hours in a world-class infrastructure versus traveling for days in a sub-standard and crowded Indian Railways system.

Since India has an extensive and effective railway infrastructure already in place, the choice to sell it to private enterprise would benefit India's citizens, especially when the role of government would be to work as a referee to make sure the competition is managed for consumers' benefit. India's train stations could be as glamorous and productive as its most successful malls. If managed properly, India's railway stations will become the most expensive real estate in a city to lease. One could easily envision businesses competing for the opportunity to sell their goods to the millions of daily travelers.

Considering the great number of travelers who use Indian Railways on a daily basis, privatizing India's trains, its railway stations managed by private industry, and converting its stations to some of the most prized real estate, will not only make the whole railway system extremely profitable and the envy of the rest of the world, but also boost local economies and bring much-required jobs to Indian youth. Competition by multiple train operators will increase the number of jobs in every function of these companies. Profitable companies will be able to raise capital to upgrade train coaches and make train travel more comfortable to the masses. For-profit companies will clamp down on free travel and make sure that the customers who buy the tickets do not have to share their seats with local groups who hop on without purchasing tickets. Similarly, higher revenues from stations will allow government to upgrade these stations and create a multitude of more jobs at the stations. In the end, such changes will improve train travel, make the railway industry profitable as a whole, increase employment, and grow India's GDP significantly.

h. Aviation - Why does India Need an Airline Run by the government?

Until 1990, 99.9% of Indians had never travelled in an airplane. First time I flew was when I went to the US for my graduate education. Indian Airlines and Air India were the only Indian airlines allowed to fly domestically and to international destinations. Not only was Air India more expensive than most other international airlines flying to the US, most travel agents advised me not to fly on Air India. Most people I know who have flown on Air India complain about its poor service, staff attitude, clogged toilets, and overall inferior experience when compared to other international airlines.

Even today, 95% of India's over one billion people have never flown on an airplane. Despite this, the Indian government spends billions of USD equivalent of taxpayers' money towards funding Air India and Indian Airlines. Today, 95% of India's population is subsidizing the air travel of the country's 5% richest citizens.

Since the deregulation of the airline industry in India, private airlines have done a tremendous job in competing against government-run airlines by keeping their costs low and providing much better frequency and service of air travel between major cities. As the economy continues to grow, India is expected to become one of the fastest-growing domestic markets for air travel. India should use this opportunity to allow international airlines to co-invest with India's domestic airlines to enter the international market. This will not only allow industry to add to India's GDP, but will also create jobs in the air travel industry, and in industries feeding into the air travel business.

Since there are already a number of established domestic airlines, Air India and Indian Airlines should be privatized and operated without taxpayer subsidies. Not only it is unreasonable for the government to fund these airlines from taxpayers' money, it is also counterproductive to India's overall airline industry. How can a private airline compete against such a behemoth, especially one that does not need to operate as a business? In the current system, Air India is able to dominate market share by cutting prices across routes thanks to its annual unlimited budget funded by the taxpayers. This not only adds to Air India's losses, but makes the whole domestic airline industry lose money, as other airlines then follow the same price cut to maintain their own market share.

Over the last few years, Air India has accumulated over 3 billion USD equivalent in losses, and its overall debt is close to 7.5 billion USD equivalent. This is a severe drain on taxpayer money. India could have used this money for a multitude of other purposes. Air India and Indian Airlines are integrated with other government-run companies such as Indian Oil to purchase jet fuel, or Airport Authority of India for airport facilities. Losses in Air India and Indian Airlines drag all supplier companies down, as Air India and Indian Airlines may not pay on time or not pay at all.

Air India and Indian Airlines are mostly in the news for the wrong reasons, like accidents, pilot strikes, delayed flights, and other embarrassing incidents. Indians living abroad almost never use Air India. The airline's overall service is at best average and often receives poor reviews.

Like most other government organizations, the government airlines' management is made up of government administrators who have minimal experience in the airline industry. Air India competes with a multitude of airlines in international markets run by industry experts who have years of experience to operate under market pressures to run those airlines as profitable businesses. Additionally, the airline business is a very capital-intensive business, with minimal margins for error in comparison to other commercial businesses. Airlines' profitability depends on management's decision on choosing profitable routes, type of aircraft based on the routes they fly, overall cost of operations, pricing, and finally the customer experience for travelers to use the same airline again. Most employees in a competitive industry are replaced if they are unable to grow a business profitably. Market forces allow the best talent to be hired and replaced in all roles to not only make a business profitable but to react to market conditions and grow on the expense of other poorly managed competitors.

In a government-run airline, such market forces are eliminated as government not only guarantees to fund all losses but also makes it hard to reduce costs as it guarantees job security and annual pay raises for its management and employees based on seniority rather than job performance. Additionally, if government has to fund multiple loss-making businesses across the wide spectrum of running a country, it is not able to provide capital as and when required by all these businesses. That makes all of these individual businesses, especially the ones that require large capital investments like airlines, uncompetitive in their industries. This fuels further losses across all government-run businesses, and loss of market position forces low employee morale across the whole organization. Guaranteed job security and compensation adds an uncaring attitude by the employees, adding further losses to these businesses. This is an unending cycle. Privatizing the airlines and bringing in professional management with long experience running an airline profitably is the only solution to reverse these losses.

Since other private airlines now provide a large network for flights to major Indian, and a number of International cities, Air India and Indian Airlines must be added to the list of government-funded companies from which government must exit and let them compete in the private industry on their own. Government should invite other airlines to purchase both Indian Airlines and Air India operations. If none of the other airlines are interested in a purchase, then government should sell its stock in the open stock market. The new shareholders will hire professional management and demand profitability for their investment.

Government should focus on upgrading India's major airports and selectively build the next set of airports only when market demand requires it. Even today, as I travel to India, one can find stray dogs just outside the New Delhi's International Arrivals Terminal. Embarrassingly, the main exit road out of the New Delhi airport is full of potholes. This surely does not bode well for any foreign investor or visitor looking at India as an investment or a tourist destination. Government's role in aviation should be making sure that airlines follow strict safety standards and airports are built and maintained to international standards. Construction, improvement, and airport infrastructure maintenance should all be outsourced to private companies. Government should look at all aspects of aviation and remove unnecessary regulations wherever possible. One such regulation is the price of jet fuel. Wherever possible, government should reduce or remove surcharges to reduce the cost of air travel. Reducing cost of air travel will enable more and more people to travel by air as long-distance road and rail travel in India is not only inconvenient but also takes unreasonably long times due to poor infrastructure. That will in turn enable the government to collect more money in taxes from a larger base of air travelers to maintain, build, and upgrade airport facilities in additional cities across India. Lastly, India should allow domestic companies to fly internationally to further increase their profitability, and hire more employees as international routes are much more profitable for most airlines.

By continuing with the right deregulation policies, fair competition, and the privatization of Air India and Indian Airlines, air travel can be made accessible to India's middle class. It is possible that over the next ten years, air travel can be used by up to 25% percent of India's population. This can be achieved by a combination of lowering air ticket prices, enabling a larger population to achieve higher incomes, job growth, and a fair and friendly business environment in India. To make that happen, government must sell its Air India and Indian Airlines stakes to investors and competing airlines, and use the money to improve India's airports to international standards and build new airports in the next set of growing cities— thereby again increasing India's GDP and increasing employment in the overall aviation and tourism industries.

i. Defense: Build Domestically. One Hundred Billion is a Lot of Money to Give to Other Countries to Defend India.

India currently has over 4.2 million personnel in its active and reserve defense forces. It has over 2,100 aircraft, 295 naval vessels, and 130 nuclear missiles. India's archrival Pakistan has 951 aircraft, 197 naval vessels, and a significant number of nuclear weapons. Pakistan is expected to spend 8.78 billion USD on its defense budget. To the north, China has almost 2.3 million personnel in its armed forces and is expected to spend over 233 billion USD equivalent on its defense infrastructure and personnel. Given India has fought wars with both Pakistan and China in the past, and India's relationship with both Pakistan and China have remained tense, India is forced to continue to strengthen and modernize its defense forces. India's defense budget for 2017 is over 53.5 billion USD.

India is at a pivotal crossroads. India can choose to remain on the road it has taken for the last seventy years, or it can detour and build a new India in the twenty-first century. India can either continue to buy weapon systems from Russia, Europe, the US, and Israel, building their economies and leaving India's future generations with financial debt, or India can call on its best and brightest to build the next generation of weapon systems. India must set aside up to 20% of its defense budgets to buy its next generation weapon systems from its domestic companies and build an ecosystem to develop its next generation weapons systems internally.

Over the last fifty years, India has invested heavily in building a system to find and train the best engineering minds in the world. India's engineers make significant contributions to worldwide innovations and economies, including NASA and most engineering Fortune 500 companies around the world. Over the last thirty years, Indian-trained engineers have founded engineering companies that have produced billions of dollars in value and tens of thousands of jobs around the world. If India offers them the opportunity and the right motivations, these engineers will build the best possible weapon systems to defend India against any aggressors.

In the centuries that Britain ruled the world, their power came from their ability to build the best naval ships and advanced weaponry of their time. Similarly, the US and their allies won both world wars thanks to the superiority of their weapons systems over those of the German and Japanese militaries.

India must develop its own weapon systems by investing in domestic engineering and production. India cannot continue to buy F-16's from the US or Rafale fighter planes from France, or Kamov helicopters from Russians, especially with the consideration that buying such weapons would require capital that India does not really have. For a country where nearly half of the population cannot afford their daily meals, it is absurd to spend 20% of its GDP buying foreign weapons that could be produced domestically at thirty percent of the cost. In order to become a nation that the world admires, India has to innovate to develop and build the best technology for use in air, land, and naval defense. Not only do such purchases remove opportunities to develop technologies in India, it also creates opportunities of large-scale corruption across all military purchases. India currently is dealing with multiple such corruption inquires going back to the 1980s.

Indian laws should be amended so that the government cannot purchase weapon systems from foreign companies using taxpayers' money after a certain date in the future. Initially, companies should be allowed to build in partnership with non-Indian companies, but any company signing up for such contracts must be given a time line to produce 100% of that weapon system locally. India's government should invest in developing a domestic system that allows outsourcing to local private sectors to build India's armaments. Similar systems are developed and put in place in the US, France, Britain, and Russia that have functioned well over the last seventy-five years. India might be a few decades late, but given its talent India can easily meet the advancements of these countries within the next twenty years if it acts quickly.

j. Tourism and India's Historical Monuments.

Every historical civilization has left dazzling monuments as a mark to record their time and achievements on Earth. The task of future generations is to respect and maintain these monuments as a way of preserving the legacy and achievements of their ancestors and their history. All of the world's oldest civilizations, such as the Greeks, Egyptians, Europeans, and Chinese have worked hard to maintain their historical monuments, both as symbols of past achievements as well as a means for huge revenue streams and employment through tourism.

The history, culture, and monuments of India are unparalleled to anything in the world. With monuments like the Taj Mahal, Ajanta Caves, Konark and Banaras's temples, Buddha's birthplace, and the innumerable forts and temples that were built before the advent of the Western calendar, India has unmatched potential for tourism. Additionally, India offers unique geographical diversity, from the panoramic Himalayan vistas, its pristine coastline with spectacular beaches, and its vast deserts. India is a tourism gold mine, capable of bringing in hundreds of billions in USD equivalent in tourism revenues. The tourism industry alone is capable of funding all of India's infrastructure needs.

Today, tourism makes up over 10% of the world economy. For a number of countries around the world, tourism has become their top revenue-generating industry. For example, in 2014 the US earned 1.4 trillion USD from tourists. European countries like France, Italy, Spain and the UK earn billions of dollars from 50 -100 million tourists every year. Twenty percent of Thailand's GDP is made up of tourism revenues. China has spent money to make tourism its key industry and is expected to become the largest tourist revenue generator in the world. India is currently ranked fortieth in worldwide tourist destination with only 8 million people visiting India every year. If that number were to increase to 50 million tourists per year, it would create millions of new jobs across construction, hospitality, transportation and food industries. Such a tourist industry would also add over a minimum of 100 billion USD to 500 billion USD equivalent annually to India's GDP.

Unfortunately, India is slowly losing its monuments and historical architecture to neglect, corruption, and the passage of time. It is really unfortunate that the potential of the tourism industry has been long neglected by India's policy makers. The Taj Mahal, India's best-known architectural site, is yellowing because of the poorly placed refinery nearby. The Taj Mahal's floors are almost worn out due to the high level of foot traffic. Other great monuments like the Red Fort, Delhi's Jama Masjid, and Fatehpur Sikri near Agra and the Char Minar in Hyderabad, plus numerous other monuments, are almost lost due to an absence of well-planned tourism policy and lack of resources for their upkeep.

The lack of a comprehensive tourism policy, poor transportation infrastructure, massive deforestation, and severe pollution, has a significantly negative impact on tourism in India. Major tourist destinations such as Ooty and Marine Drive in Bombay are now polluted beyond recognition. Why would one visit Ooty, where the lake looks black and trash fills the landscape, or Bombay's Marine Drive filled with trash and the water polluted by industrial waste, when one can visit Europe, Australia, or the US, where the cities are clean, monuments are preserved, and the local transportation provides an easy access to all tourist spots in the city? It is much easier for tourists to travel in the air-conditioned comfortable train network in Europe than waiting for a train on a trash-filled, overcrowded, hot and muggy railway station in India, which may be running a few hours late. Even though India's Himalayan mountain range offers the best panoramic and majestic views, the basic road and transport infrastructure needs a major investment to attract the same tourist away from similar destination in the Alps in Europe or the Rocky Mountains in the US. Today, millions of tourists travelling to the Caribbean, coastal cities across Europe, South America, and Australia could visit India if similar investments are made in the infrastructure and cleanliness of Indian cities located on India's large coastline.

Personally, it was unbelievable to see that the international tourist destinations shown in Indian cinema are really as beautiful in reality as I saw them in films growing up in India. On a visit to Rome, it reminded me of India, being an old civilization with historic monuments. It was an incredible experience to see that the shop owners in each Roman marketplace washed the whole square every evening; tables with freshly-cut flowers were set out in the middle of the piazza for tourists to dine, while someone played live music in the piazza. I wondered why it could not be done in India on a summer evening, until I visited a major marketplace outside Delhi. The marketplace had the same setting, shops set in a square area with corridors, but with unauthorized sellers selling toys, magazines, and other trinkets. The main restaurant in India's marketplace allowed its guests to eat standing in the corridor and let the trash pile up right in front of the restaurant. In the middle of the square, similar to where I had seen a musician play violin on the summer evening in Rome, India's marketplace had used the same space as a parking lot, where people drove dangerously with no regard for others. Just a visit to this marketplace was enough to see why a tourist would visit Rome over Delhi for a vacation.

Not only must India invest in its infrastructure and maintenance of its historical monuments, it needs to also invest significantly in its basic law and order infrastructure. Frequent news of crimes against women in India makes it harder for international tourists to choose India as their first holiday destination.

For India to attract foreign and domestic tourists alike and create a 100 billion USD equivalent tourism industry, India must invest in its highways, railway stations, airports; must privatize inter, intra-state, and local transportation; reform overall law and order, including traffic, parking, and crime in its cities; and make the required changes in environmental protection and reforms required in trash collection and recycling to keep its cities clean.

To promote tourism, India's tourism ministry should identify India's top 1,000 monuments and then outsource their upkeep to private companies. Ticket prices and local taxes should be enacted and collected to support the high level of upkeep required by the monuments. The tourism industry should also work with private banks and local governments to fund and facilitate the opening of boutique hotels across the country by local entrepreneurs. Each hotel and restaurant should add a surcharge to support the upkeep of local monuments. City mayors and local business leaders should be made responsible to simplify local transportation to make their cities attractive to tourism. All restaurants must be certified and regularly checked to reduce incidences of food-related illness.

India's breathtaking monuments and historic sites, its mountains, beaches and deserts, along with its beautiful and mysterious story of centuries of civilization, should make India a top destination for the world to visit. India's culture, it's changing of languages and gods from place to place, should make it a dream vacation place for people around the world. But unless India is able to clean up its cities, remove pollution, make it easy to travel between and within cities, and work hard to restore its monuments, it will be very difficult to compete against Paris, London, Rome, Athens, New York, Las Vegas, Orlando, or numerous other cities in Europe, the Caribbean, Thailand, and China, who do offer everything a tourist is looking for in a dream vacation.

Lastly, today, a large aging population around the world is looking for places with a cheaper cost of living and good quality of life to retire. If India can do all these reforms to make India a great tourist destination, its low cost of living would also make India one of the top destinations for people to retire. Such a move would not only create thousands of new jobs in India's real estate, healthcare, and other service industries, but also add millions to India's GDP.

k. Medical Tourism: India Must Become the World's Hospital.

In Indian culture, children aspire to become either a doctor or an engineer when they grow up. Children spend the first eighteen years of their life chasing that goal. Almost half of India's best and brightest students choose medicine as their profession. As a result, India produces over 50,000 doctors every year, and currently has over a million doctors practicing medicine. Until the 1990s, most Indian doctors worked in government hospitals or ran local practices. Since the government has allowed industry to open private hospitals, it has created tens of thousands of jobs in the medical profession.

Even with a million registered doctors, because of its large population India still lags behind developed countries around the world for doctors per 1,000 people. Currently India has 0.6 doctors per 1,000 people, in comparison to China with 1.8 doctors, and the US with 2.5 doctors per 1,000 people. As part of improving education programs, government should allow tax breaks for private investors to invest in opening additional medical colleges and nursing schools. Government should create a separate agency to regulate education in all medical colleges and institutes, providing clear guidelines for its coursework, equipment, and facilities, in order to provide a quality education in all medical fields, including bachelors in medicine, nursing, and other related programs. This agency should set and regularly update national standards for all related fields as these students hold the power of life and death of their patients in their hands.

Today, thousands of Indian citizens living abroad, and foreigners too, are reaching out to India's private hospitals in search of affordable and quality health care. Modern-day India is on the brink of a new industry bigger than software exports and outsourcing combined: providing quality health care. As international health care costs are increasing at a tremendous pace, India is able to provide quality health care services at a fraction of the cost of American and European hospitals. The same open-heart surgery operation that may cost 15,000 USD in the US can be done for 1,500 USD equivalent in India. An overnight stay in a US hospital can cost over $15,000. India can provide the same quality of care for less than 500 USD equivalent per day. Such price differentials, if managed with proper care, can bring millions of patients from all over the world to India mostly for its quality healthcare.

Today, due to the increased life expectancy in most Western countries, health care costs are rapidly becoming unaffordable. India is on the precipice of leading the world in providing health care. India must encourage the Indian private healthcare industry to invest in state-of-the-art hospitals; elderly care homes; specialized medicine for children; and research centers in order to lead the world in health care. India already has the doctors, nurses, and inherent talent to provide these important services on a global scale.

India's private hospitals, as part of their licenses to offer medical services, must be required to work with India's medical colleges to provide training, residencies, and hiring opportunities to students graduating from these medical schools to, first, maintain quality, and secondly, bring the additional doctors required to expand India's growing healthcare industry.

India's government should slowly allow private hospitals to mostly take over the business of medicine. Government hospitals should only be available for people below a certain income level, and government employees, providing medicine at minimal cost to citizens living below poverty levels.

A government agency must be created as an oversight much a like utility commission over the private medical industry, with state and regional offices to make sure that hospitals' service offerings are priced reasonably. All personnel working in the oversight agency must declare their assets annually. Any misreporting must carry severe fines, including long prison sentences.

Another government agency, similar to the FDA in the US, should be created to monitor new therapies, disseminate research, and act on national, statewide, and regional medical emergencies. This agency should also be provided regulatory powers to approve new drugs or therapies from private companies to be sold to the general public.

Private hospitals should offer a required number of hours per physician to help people below a certain income level. Additionally, private hospitals, as part of the business opportunities provided to them, should become part of a public-private partnership and be required to pay towards a local fund to help government hospitals based on the number of doctors it employs. Private hospitals should be encouraged to work with medical colleges and the pharmaceutical industry to develop new therapies and drugs.

To help bridge the shortage of doctors in India, all medical students must be required to spend at least three months in their last year of medical school working in government hospitals. As India's rural areas have been neglected for the longest time, such requirement must be made as part of the medicine curriculum to graduate from the medical school.

India has a long history of Ayurveda medicine. India's day-to-day medical culture is based on practices of Ayurveda passed on to families over generations. In the modern world, Ayurveda offers remedies capable of solving medical ailments that the West is just beginning to investigate. Ayurveda has brought Yoga to the world, and it lists medicines to reduce blood pressure, cholesterol, and diabetes, as well as other remedies to major health ailments. The many patients of Ayurvedic medicine vouch for its effectiveness and minimal side effects, both of which separate it from Western medicine. Colleges must be required to offer courses and accredited programs in Ayurvedic medicine. If required, it must be funded from taxes received from healthcare providers across the country. Ayurveda has the power to become a major branch of medicine as it has been practiced in India for thousands of years. It can open the fields of medical research and huge job opportunities for India's youth to pursue the research and practice of Ayurveda.

Overall investment in medical schools, private hospitals, and medical homes for the elderly, can generate millions of new jobs. At the same time, the need for cheaper medical care around the world can add trillions of USD equivalent to India's GDP. The Indian government, working with the medical industry, should extensively promote India's medical care. India's private health care industry should partner with other industries, such as -tourism and public relations, to take its message of India's high quality, low-cost health care to the whole world.

1. Manufacturing: Let's Save it Before India Becomes China's Slave.

Manufacturing has changed the fortunes of nations and created affluent societies around the world for a long time. The rise of the British, Spanish, American, and Chinese nations was all powered by manufacturing prowess of armament, naval, and industrial manufacturing revolutions. Manufacturing allows masses of people to be employed, and harnesses their efforts in building products that can change the fortunes of countries and its people. Even though automation has made it difficult for countries to build new manufacturing bases based on large labor pools, India could be the last bastion of the manufacturing industry to create wealth for its people. India has youth, a large population, and the basic training infrastructure in place to build a manufacturing base.

In most labor intensive, non-skilled manufacturing industries such as furniture making, electronic goods, toys, and home goods, with its large population, significant investment in manufacturing technology, and their government's ability to control wages, China has become the low cost leader in the world market. It would be foolish for India's policy makers to build similar low cost products in competition with China for international markets. On the other spectrum, the US, Germany, and Japan lead the world in manufacturing using automation. It would also be difficult for India to reach technology sophistication to compete directly with them using automation for the same products.

First and foremost, India's policy makers must work to protect its manufacturing industry for domestic consumption from Chinese products. China is currently exporting over 60 billion USD equivalent in products to India, ranging from mobile phones, electrical goods and machinery, and importing 10 billion USD equivalent of raw materials such as ores, cotton, and minerals. The last time such a practice was common was when the British ruled India. The British took the raw materials from India, built the finished products in the United Kingdom, and sold them back to India for tidy profits. If India does not fix such lopsided trade practices, it will kill all India's manufacturing ambitions before they even get started.

As a policy, India should stop exports of its raw materials altogether. Each industry that could be flooded by foreign imports by low cost products must be evaluated and should only be opened to foreign products as and when local industry is allowed to establish itself in the domestic market. Companies who are aided by their government through state subsidies and artificial low manufacturing wages must be banned from selling their products in India. If India's policy makers do not take the right steps in protecting these industries, India will never be able to build a manufacturing base even to supply to its domestic market.

India's policy makers should identify industries for exports that are uniquely suited for India's inherent talent. Since India is uniquely able to produce engineering talent, India must focus on industries where engineering talent could be used to develop and build products for domestic and international markets. The next generation of automobile technologies, audio-visual technologies, smart home technologies, alternative power source equipment, and other similar products that require a large technical workforce, must be evaluated and selected for manufacturing. India's policy makers should look at Samsung, LG, Hyundai, and Kia Motors from South Korea and HTC from Taiwan for inspiration when selecting industries and manufacturing products in India.

Given the low per capita income of its consumers, India should encourage investment by local entrepreneurs and companies in industries that may have large rural consumption. For example, creating a national policy to replace all paper products with earthenware or products made by organic materials, or finding other materials to replace paper products, could create a large number of new manufacturing jobs. Similarly, replacing all plastic bags with cloth bags will not only help to create new jobs, it will also help in reducing trash produced from paper and plastic products.

To promote manufacturing, India must simplify its land acquisition laws so entrepreneurs and investors can invest in manufacturing. Additionally, India needs to build public-private partnerships to train millions of its youth with manufacturing skills. Today, there are very few private institutes providing quality training for jobs such as electricians, auto mechanics, computer-aided designers, metal welders, carpenters, masons, plumbers, electronic and mechanical parts repair, and a multitude of similar jobs required in the manufacturing industry.

Government should simplify India's tax code and provide significant tax breaks to encourage foreign investors to build a manufacturing base in India and help export to other countries. With easy access to ports, an English-speaking young and educated population is very desirable for a lot of international companies provided government makes the process of doing business in India easier. Even today, India has arduous regulations, paperwork, corruption and an almost circular bureaucracy inhibiting international companies who might consider India as a manufacturing base.

All government agencies must be asked to buy local, whether these are raw materials such as steel, cement, fertilizers or the finished products such as automobiles, office equipment, trucks, cars or similar products.

Processes to provide bank loans should be made easier to established companies with strong balance sheets. Government, through its central banks, should encourage private banks to offer low-interest loans for companies looking to grow the manufacturing base.

India should create a ministry of manufacturing to not just review all the existing regulations but also to help the private sector create a national target for jobs to be created. This ministry should be tasked to define a national manufacturing policy to create up to 20% of the total jobs target through manufacturing in the next ten years. It should look at various industries and decide which should be protected for domestic growth and which should be opened for international investment. The ministry of manufacturing should have a mandate to make sure both employers' and employees' issues are raised at the national level; should work with both sides to eliminate arcane laws, enforce existing laws, and help write new laws to fairly protect all groups involved in the manufacturing industry; and should act as a referee for the overall industry in making sure that employer and employee rights are protected.

Today, India's labor force works in horrific conditions without any oversight or action from the government. Employers are able to bribe authorities to look the other way, forcing manufacturing employees to work under hazardous working conditions. Enforcement by federal authorities must be added to remove corrupt officials.

In a personal experience of visiting a small manufacturing supplier to the automobile industry, I met with the owner in his air-conditioned office with a plush carpet, and comfortable and elegant furnishings. When I visited the factory, fifty of the company employees worked in an unbearably hot, dark, and congested factory floor as they welded various pieces of metal together to build seats for scooters and motorcycles. I am 100% sure that the working conditions on the factory floor did not meet the required working conditions and safety standards. The government, as referee, is required to make sure that such factories are monitored and penalized for such flagrant abuse of its employees, but I am also sure that the owner was able to bribe the government inspector to overlook the safety standards and approve the factory to operate, which forced the factory workers to work in hazardous conditions without any recourse.

In summary, government must ban export of all raw materials, limit import of products, which are subsidized by a foreign government and simplify starting of a manufacturing business in India by international companies. Just by protecting the manufacturing base for domestic consumption in cell phones, solar power, home building materials such as cement, tiles, fixtures and home appliances, televisions, automobile and day-to-day low tech manufacturing can create millions of new jobs and add billions of USD equivalent to India's GDP. India should create a ministry in identifying and assisting private industry to develop products in the manufacturing industry. A ministry of manufacturing should work to protect rights of employers and employees, and simplify all impediments to making a strong manufacturing base in order to create up to 20% of all new jobs over the next ten years.

m. Software Development and Outsourcing.

India has become one of the world leaders in software development and back-end outsourced operations for a large number of companies. Major corporations such as Microsoft, Google, Oracle, SAP, Amazon, and numerous other Fortune 500 companies have opened development centers in major cities in India, employing thousands of developers. Such software development and outsourcing of back-end tasks has allowed India to create hundreds of thousands of jobs. Most of this success can be attributed to India's education system prioritizing math and science education to its large number of primary and secondary school students.

Like any industry, India must protect its lead in software development and outsourcing by investing in school, college, and university curriculums and equipment, and teaching computer programming to kids as early as primary school. As computers are now an integral part of daily life, most developed and developing countries have introduced computer programming to their children earlier and earlier.

India will see competition for such jobs around the world from the native countries where India sends its programmers today, as well as from developing countries that see it a lucrative field to add to their GDP. Over the last decade, China has invested heavily in English language education and is becoming a serious competitor to India in offshore software development model. A number of ex-USSR countries have emerged as a strong base for software developers as well. Companies in the US and European Union are looking at these countries to outsource software development not only due to proximity and better infrastructure, but also as wages in India have risen year-over-year in the last decade.

Even though Indian companies are now developing products for the Indian domestic market, as well as building software for large-scale government projects to systematically introduce technology in government operations, India is far behind in bringing innovative products to marketplace. In the top 100 software product companies by revenue, none of these companies were started in India. All innovation in the software industry, and all new software products, is still led by countries like the US, Germany and other developed countries.

For India to continue to lead the world in software development, India's leading companies must ask its business leadership to change the mindset of their employees. Company leaders should turn these companies into the next generation of innovators rather than staying a back-end development shop. Business leaders must create a reward system for their employees to spawn new products within or outside their companies. Sooner rather than later, other companies around the world will catch up to do the back-end work of testing and tabulation by automation at a cheaper price currently done by India.

India must simplify the process of starting a software business, strengthen copyright and other intellectual property protection laws, provide tax breaks and financial incentives for software developers and companies to build products that could bring India to the forefront of software product innovation. Software product innovation is still happening in countries like the US and Germany, and Indian developers are working as contract labor to build these products, but there is no reason why the next generation of search engine or operating systems or browser software could not be conceived and built in India.

Unfortunately, for individual entrepreneurs to succeed in India, it is still difficult to acquire venture capital financing, copyright protections, a defense of intellectual property, or laws that protect and help employers to create and sustain these businesses. In the early 2000s, a large number of successful US venture capital firms set up offices in India, and on average invested 200 million USD in various companies. By 2015, most of these firms had exited India due to severe losses. Unless the right business environment and protections are provided, innovation and growth is difficult. All the software developers being churned out now from India's private engineering colleges will see high unemployment over the next decade.

India should use its tremendous software manpower to build transparency in the functioning of its government. India must bring its police, legal, education, social services, tax filings, healthcare and other day-to-day services provided by the government on-line and connect them to eliminate corruption, increase accountability, and ensure the smooth functioning of the government. India should hire its large software development companies to build easy-to-use, world-class systems, thereby making the functioning of India's government transparent and removing corruption from every level of the government in the process.

Government must outsource all software development to India's large software development companies to build user-friendly websites. Unfortunately, at the moment India continues to use a government-employee model to build its software solutions for government services like applications for identity cards, tax payments, rail reservations, airline bookings, and other day-to-day services where the government interacts with the public directly. All these websites and systems do not inspire confidence in the government's ability to build large-scale software systems. User experience in most of these systems is generally poor and cumbersome. In a few personal experiences using these websites, it reminded me of similar frustration when I had to interact with Indian banks and government offices to do simple transactions. It is almost absurd that the world's largest software development outsourcer country's websites are clunky. Using these websites feels like they are designed and developed by a high school student.. These websites should only be launched when they are functional and easy to use.

In summary, India must protect its lead in the software development and software outsourcing industry by first improving the quality of institutes graduating its next generation of computer science graduates, as well as exposing its students early to computer science for them to become interested in becoming computer developers at an early age. Additionally, India must invest in creating the right environment and providing the right eco-system, such as raising capital, ease of company formation, labor and tax laws, and protections such as copyrights and intellectual property, for all those involved in software development to create innovative products that can succeed at the International level. Such an eco-system would turn India from a contract developer to a culture of creating innovative products. All software development for government needs must be outsourced to build the best class of software interactions between the government and its public users.

India has just started to deploy software technology in its day-to-day tasks of bill payments, navigation, and basic conveniences made available by the Internet. India has been an adopter rather than an inventor in this cycle of software development and innovation. With the next generation of software development applications such as machine learning, data science, artificial intelligence, health science, quantum computing, and Internet of Things (IoT), and other new fields opened every day by people around the world, India is well positioned to take a leadership position provided the right approach and policy is formulated by the government today. With the right policy framework, software development alone can create millions of new jobs, add billions of USD equivalent to India's GDP, and help reduce poverty from India's masses.

n. Space Industry: Let's Use it as a Job Creator.

Unlike most other government-funded programs, after a significant investment, India has done well in developing a successful space program. Its results are now well documented in weather forecasting, communications, and defense programs. India's space program has become the brightest shining star in India's overall success story. Today, India has one of the most respected space programs in the world. It is now entering into commercial relationships to launch satellites for other private companies and countries around the world. But like any other government-controlled organization, India's space program is funded by taxpayer money.

But a philosophical question can be raised. Does it make sense for a country that cannot provide clean water, air, or food to its citizens to build a space program? Does it matter if India can send a probe to Mars to study it?

Given India's space research organizations are funded by the government and has been a research organization for decades, there is no financial accountability of such organizations. One can justify India's space program investment by looking at returns in the advancements made in communications and defense programs. At this juncture, as it takes large amounts of financial investments, any other usage of space technology other than defense must be licensed to private companies to further advance these technologies. Such a policy will not only make these projects financially efficient, it will also expedite the time line of the next set of goals set by India's space organization, and create thousands of new jobs. Such technology licensing must be done under the guidance of the space research program. The space research program should set the agenda and guide the direction of overall projects. Such a private-public partnership in space programs will create jobs and speed up the overall program targets.

In the US, NASA and the US defense department have used such successful private-public partnerships for years in building the best technologies for space exploration and the US defense department. Most of the US defense development of fighter aircraft, submarines, aircraft carriers, missiles, and other technologies, are done and built by private companies such as Boeing, McDonald Douglas, Lockheed Martin, General Dynamics, Northrop Grumman, and many other private defense contractor companies. Similarly, NASA is now outsourcing to companies like Boeing and Space X for the next generation of space technologies. It took NASA billions of dollars to send out satellites in space in the 1960s. Companies like Space X are able to launch satellites at one-thousandth the cost of NASA, and it took one-fiftieth the time of NASA to launch satellites in space. Private companies, if brought as partners with India's space program, can further reduce the cost of a rocket launch by making its space satellite launch one of the cheapest programs in world. This will also enable these companies to generate large number of jobs in India and compete for satellite launch business from developing countries.

India's space program should be mandated to focus on major national issues such as weather forecasting, environmental studies like global warming, the receding of Himalayan glaciers, changing rain patterns, and defense-related technologies such as missile systems to keep the country safe.

India's government-funded space program should limit its focus of fundamental research and outsource all experimentation and implementation of technology to private companies. Other commercial aspects of the space program from communications and other discovery should be brought into a public-private partnership, as India must use its taxpayers' money to more pressing problems of education, housing, and feeding its citizens.

o. Traffic: Reduce it, Streamline it, or India will Remain a Third World Country.

Considering transportation systems are the arteries of any economy, helping the flow of goods, people, and business across the system, to build large economies most developed countries first invested heavily in building state-of-the-art roads, highways, rails, ports and airports.

It is equally important to make sure that these transport systems are efficient. Efficient transport contributes significantly to a country's GDP by saving travel time for its people and making them more productive at their workplace. Efficient transport of goods also reduces inflation, helping a country to produce more and add to the country's GDP.

Today, India not only lacks a state-of-the-art transportation system, India's transportation systems are highly inefficient due to the lack of enforcement of traffic laws across the country. It can easily take hours to go ten kilometers by road during commuting hours in its major cities. A few years ago, during a trip to India, I agreed to attend a wedding just outside of East Delhi. The wedding invitation said 7 PM. Since the travel distance was fifty kilometers, I started at 5 PM to make sure I could be there by the scheduled time. I took the fastest route, using the Outer Ring Road, a forty-seven kilometer long highway built in 1984 surrounding the city of Delhi to bypass the traffic going between the surrounding states. As soon as I reached the Outer Ring Road, I got the first impression of India's traffic woes. The four-lane highway was as packed as a parking lot as people drove in eight different lanes without any semblance of civilized traffic behavior. Everyone was honking as if others were not aware of the traffic congestion, as if by honking it would open up a new lane for each person.

In a similar traffic jam during daily commuting hours outside Washington DC on the beltway, equivalent to Delhi's Outer Ring Road, people drove in specified lanes for traffic to clear-up. It is not that people living in Washington, DC, are more civilized or only seldom face traffic problems; it is the fear that if they misbehave and someone does call a traffic cop, they will get a hefty fine and it will increase their monthly insurance. A simple traffic ticket will cost that driver $1,000 in overall penalties.

By the time I reached the wedding, it was 10:30 PM. Not only was the wedding over, most guests had already left. A fifty kilometer-drive in 5.5 hours! A recent traffic study suggests that the average speed in Delhi is now five kilometers per hour during commuting hours. Such delays are mostly caused due to lack of infrastructure in relation to the number of vehicles on the road, and the lack of enforcement of its traffic rules. Lots of drivers currently on the roads have not been properly trained and have obtained driver's licenses by bribing government officials. Recent reports suggest that in some states as many as 6 out of 10 driver's licenses are issued to drivers without them even taking a driving test. There is hardly any political will or civic urgency for people to follow traffic rules. As a result, India not only has one of the most chaotic and inefficient traffic systems, it has one of the highest traffic accident rates in the developing world. India had over 489,000 traffic accidents and 180,000 deaths in traffic accidents in 2015. According to a WHO report, India had over 130 deaths per 100,000 vehicles in 2013. In comparison, the US had twelve deaths per 100,000 vehicles. It continues to get worse as millions of new cars and other vehicles are sold every year. This state of affairs has led to India's roads being extremely dangerous. Most drivers, including those who have been trained, do not follow traffic rules. On any given two-lane road, it is common to see drivers travelling in multiple lanes without any regard to traffic rules. Red lights seem to have no effect in smaller intersections, and drunk driving is all too common. Cars going against the direction of traffic can be witnessed on highways and major city roads.

Most Indian cities lack basic traffic infrastructure. There is no concept of stop signs, and people honk endlessly, adding to chaos and dramatic sound pollution. Often, traffic lights do not work for days. People take U-turns for convenience, holding up traffic on busy roads. Pedestrian crossings, bicycle lanes, bus and truck lanes—all of which are common in many highly populated countries—do not exist in India.

In order for India to develop into a major developed economy over the next twenty years, traffic must be reduced and streamlined. Central and state governments must work together to create unified traffic legislation that results in one hundred percent of driver's licenses issued legitimately, and implement penalties to enforce traffic laws. For future highway and intra-city traffic, first priority must the given to create bus lanes to promote the use of public transportation. To this end, cities should also enforce a car curfew during business hours. This will not only reduce urban traffic, but will also diminish the pollution that threatens the health of all people living in Indian cities. State government should require the installation of basic necessities, including traffic infrastructure like red lights and stop signs at every cross-section. The government should make use of red light cameras to issue speeding tickets on major intersections, which in turn must be paid by their due date. Failure to pay a ticket should result in the suspension of the driver's license and vehicle registration. Such information of suspended driver licenses and registrations should also be readily available to traffic police in real time. The funds received from such enforcement should be put towards connecting traffic police countrywide with state-of-the-art communications systems to catch repeat offenders across city or state borders. Lastly, India should pass legislation to remove all sorts of horns or similar devices from all of its vehicles. Any such devices in vehicles must carry significant fines.

Today, people do not follow the traffic rules because they know they can get out of any violation by bribing traffic police. Major investment must be made in technologies such as body and car cameras for all traffic police to make sure they are not able to take a bribe, and that all interactions with the public is recorded. Any traffic police personnel found accepting bribes should be terminated from the job. At the same time, India must employ an adequate number of traffic police personnel to manage traffic in its mega-cities. A national standard of traffic police personnel per 1,000 vehicles must be set by a traffic police study, and all cities and states must be required to adhere to such standards.

The Indian government must create special courts to hear traffic violations, and new legislation should mandate a time frame for traffic violations to be legally closed. Repeat offenders should be punished with fines and imprisonment for incidents that lead to serious injuries or death. Furthermore, a national traffic violation system should be created and should be accessible to all private insurance companies for an access fee. This will force the insurance rates of repeat offenders to increase, which in some cases might force them off the roads. Driving on public infrastructure is a privilege, not a right.

City governments should be enabled to introduce taxes and collect funds by various means, including issuing bonds to raise money for the improvement of local transportation systems—like adding trams, metro trains, or private local buses to reduce and streamline traffic at a city level.

Interstate public transportation should be privatized and regulated by a national regulatory body. State government should sell their buses at auction and allow private companies to lease and manage local bus stations. All private transportation companies would pay a fee for their use. These fees would be used to maintain the bus station infrastructure, with the same model being proposed for interstate railways as is currently used for the airports across the country.

Since 99% of India's population travels on buses and trains, government should make sure that all bus stations and railways stations are built to international standards and provide the same quality of services to its citizens. If airports can be built to that quality, India can do the same for its bus and railway stations. The government must create a national regulatory body with ample authority to solve India's interstate transportation issues within the next five years. The national regulatory body would oversee all such private transportation companies. Any late arrivals or failure to service routes should be reviewed on weekly, monthly, and quarterly intervals. Companies not able to maintain standards must be fined under a contractual agreement or should be replaced.

Before these changes can be put in place, India must recognize the extent of its transportation management problems, and should list transportation among the country's top five urgent issues. India must invite private industry to manage and run its transport infrastructure, as its poor transport management system is hurting the quality of life of its people, and its GDP.

p. **Sports and India's Place in the World.**

Since the advent of civilization, competitive sports have been an integral part of human culture. The Greeks organized the Olympics, Egyptians loved wrestling and athletics, and every other successful civilization invented unique sports for its people. Sports are an important part of growth in a civilization.

In the modern era, successful world economies tend to lead the world in sporting competitions. Producing world-class athletes is a source of great national pride. Competitions provide opportunities for countries to demonstrate their growth in human endeavors, and produce financial opportunities and employment for millions of its people. In every international competition, including the Olympics or World Championships in various sports, the top honors are bestowed upon American, Russian, Chinese and European athletes. India, even though it makes up twenty percent of world population, remains largely unrepresented in international sports.

It is not the case that people living in the US, Europe, Russia, and China are genetically better that allows them to excel in sports. Their success can be traced to public policy, investment in sports infrastructure, and financial rewards, all of which motivate a large number of their citizens to take up sports as a career and develop themselves as world-class athletes. In the United States, starting from middle and high schools, professional coaching staffs with experience in coaching at various levels are hired by schools to train students. Additionally, major investments are made in sports infrastructure, and equipment is funded by local tax dollars. Excellence in sports is further facilitated by inter-school competition, which motivates individual athletes. U.S. colleges provide large amounts of funds to build and maintain state-of-the-art sports facilities on their campuses, and offer athletic scholarships to students who excel in sports and education at the same time. These scholarships provided in a wide range of sports, including basketball, tennis, swimming, soccer, wrestling, athletics, boxing, and numerous other sports, open doors for thousands of athletes to pursue professional sports careers while at the same time helping them finance their college educations. Lastly, the majority of community colleges offer various courses in sports training and medicine for students to pursue sports-related careers.

In the US, city and state policymakers are elected to pursue growth and improvement within their local communities. To this end, each city aspires to build the best sports infrastructure possible to advance their community. Olympic-sized swimming pools, tennis courts, and parks are built to encourage children to take an early interest in sports. City parks, playgrounds, and sports infrastructures are situated near schools in order to make sporting facilities available to all children. Cities offer large tax credits and other concessions to build stadiums to attract professional teams to play for these cities. This not only allows kids to become interested in sports but also to pursue a professional career with their local sports teams. In return, cities generate revenues from ticket sales, sports merchandise, and other related revenue streams, helping cities financially.

Unfortunately, India's policy makers have neglected to invest in sports infrastructure. Sports infrastructure in schools, public parks, and even for large stadiums, is poorly funded and deteriorating. Homeless people use public parks as shelter while the local authorities turn a blind eye. The only time the Indian government considers sports infrastructure investment is when India is hosting an international competition. In these instances, the funds are allocated to build new facilities and improve existing sports infrastructure through government organizations, and like other government-funded projects, the majority of funds are distributed between the politicians and the bureaucrats and the facilities crumble before the event is even over.

As discussed before, a part of school budgets must be mandated towards sports infrastructure. Primary schools must be equipped with swings, slides, merry-go-rounds, and other similar apparatuses. Middle schools must provide basic sports infrastructure for young adults, such as running tracks, basketball, volleyball, and badminton courts, equipment for indoor sports such as table tennis, chess, and other similar sports, and playgrounds for outdoor sports such as soccer, cricket, and field hockey—along with equipment, coaching, and training staff for all these sports. High schools should make investment in facilities like Olympic-size swimming pools, gymnasiums, and tennis courts. Local city government should outsource maintenance of all public parks to private companies. Lastly, similar to the US model, cities should work with local businesses to create privately funded inter-city and inter-state sports leagues to promote professional sports. This could bring jobs and extra revenues as these companies and cities together would build the infrastructure required to promote these sports.

India has proven that if only given the proper resources and training, Indian athletes can compete with anyone in the world. India has recently produced world-class athletes in tennis, wrestling, badminton, archery, and cricket. However, considering India's large population, India can do better. If the proper facilities, equipment, and training were provided, India could produce champion athletes in all sports. Every child should have access to community pools, well-maintained parks, and coaches so that they can play soccer, hockey, or any other sports these playgrounds facilitate. At the college level, India must make sports scholarships a mandatory part of all public and private college programs. As a public policy, India's sports ministry must work hand-in-hand with the Ministry of Education to make sports education an integral part of primary, secondary, and college-level education.

India has recently instituted professional sports leagues, mainly for cricket, across various Indian cities. Similar leagues should be promoted for all team sports, including tennis, field hockey, soccer, table tennis, chess, badminton, and in as many sports as possible. The private sector should be encouraged to invest under the assumption that these could become profitable businesses. Public and private funds could go towards creating stadiums and facilities to be shared among collegiate and professional sports teams. Competitive sports should be promoted in India from primary school onwards to improve the health of the country and promote a sense of community. Public policy should be introduced that makes sports into livelihoods, from the coaches and players to the managers and stakeholders in both the private and public sector. A percentage of the country's tax revenue should be dedicated to building and maintaining playgrounds and parks. These changes are musts if India aims to improve future generations and unify the country as one people. Such investment in sports curriculum and sports infrastructure can create thousands of jobs in construction, sports training, sports medicine, and secondary jobs in supporting industries.

Chapter 8

Let's Start With the Basics: Air, Water and Food

In the twenty-first century, while developed countries are striving to land on Mars, the people of India continue to struggle with the basic necessities of life. Despite international projections that India has one of the fastest growing economies and is a force to be reckoned with, the reality of the country is very different on the ground. India is still falling short of meeting the basic needs of its population.

Furthermore, it is not merely acceptable for India's prosperous citizenry and leaders to compete with developed countries in the race to adopt the latest technology and comforts. We must also recognize that the success of these developed nations is measured by the per capita incomes and quality of life enjoyed by their average citizens and not just their technological achievements. It is a widely cited statistic that one third of the world's poorest people live in India. The majority of Indians living outside of major cities are often unable to avail themselves of even twentieth-century facilities, including basic sanitation, running water, electricity, and food. Even in the country's urban areas, the majority of the population lives in sub-human conditions. Within a hundred kilometers of any major city, India's rural population seems to be living in the nineteenth century, plagued by dilapidated infrastructure, rampant malnutrition, and extreme poverty. It is unfortunate that Indian citizens continue to live in such dire conditions. The problem is complicated by their refusal to demand change or take action. It is saddening to see India's adult population pass their pessimistic worldview on to future generations.

Time is running out for India. Within the next twenty years, India must find solutions to stimulate and generate wealth so all of its citizens can afford basic amenities. If the country fails to take the implementation of such progress seriously, it is unlikely that India will be able to continue on as a united country. Granted, the solutions to these issues will not be easy to come by, but sweeping them under the rug will not resolve them. With the invention of cable television and the Internet, the world has become extremely transparent. In order for India to join the ranks of the developed economies that India deserves to be in, India must begin by resolving the extreme poverty and inhumane conditions that the majority of India's population currently experiences. India must first focus on three basic amenities, food, water, and clean air for all Indians.

To begin with, India must provide enough money for its poor to make sure that "No child goes to bed hungry." Eighty percent of India's population earns 2 USD equivalent (Rs.125) per day. In small to major cities, hunger is extremely visible. You see small children, women, and men begging for food. India must modify its welfare model to give subsidies for basic food to its poor. India today provides food to its poor through a "ration card" system. The Ration Card program should be outsourced to private companies with government oversight. Rather than providing food such as rice, wheat, sugar, and other foods, Ration Card program should provide food coupons that can be used to buy the same food items from private food markets participating in such a program. Private food selling companies in turn should collect the money from the government, thereby eliminating the need of a parallel organization purchasing and distributing food products across the whole country. An electronic payment and tracking of coupons and delivery of food to the intended person will eliminate all possibilities of corruption. Coupons should be printed in the recipient's names, and only recipient should be able to use these coupons.

Politicians in India often court votes from the poor by providing free food. State and national governments should be prohibited from providing free food items such as rice and wheat as a political tool to gain votes except in cases of natural disasters. Providing free rice or free food to various groups for political purposes will eventually damage the country, despite the help that it may offer in the short run. Such programs, which may sound compassionate, inevitably waste taxpayers' money, and lead to increased corruption and further shortages of food. At the same time, NGOs and charitable social organizations should be allowed to raise non-taxable funds from individuals and corporations to assist those suffering from poverty and hunger. Between the food coupon program, NGOs, and charitable organizations, India must make sure that it reaches people living below the poverty line and makes food available to poor people who need assistance with the basic requirements of life.

Similarly, India must make sure that running drinking water is accessible to all of its citizens. If a country cannot even provide drinking water to all of its citizens, then the country cannot consider itself in the running to become a major world economy. India must invest in water conservation and distribution infrastructure as India is on track to become the most populous nation within the next fifteen years. In the last twenty-five years, India has seen major cities transformed into mega-cities, and even the smaller cities are unable to cope with the mass migration from an agricultural economy to an urban economy. With these changes, the shortage of running clean drinking water has become a significant issue.

With global warming projections of melting of Himalayan glaciers over the next few decades, it is further important that India creates a secondary system to provide drinking water to its large population. India must invest in infrastructure to store water locally in its village, town and cities across the country during its monsoon season, and connect these storage facilities to the water distribution systems. The government must set up a ministry and work with the private sector to resolve the current water shortage, while looking to the future and investing in long-term solutions to overcome one of the most urgent problems facing India today. The private sector should be offered heavy incentives to solve water storage and distribution network problems in India, with the aim of providing drinking water to everyone across the country.

Lastly, India has to make sure that investments are made in improving quality of air, the third basic essential of life, before other investments are made. Today's industrialization, in complete defiance of India's environmental laws, along with major deforestation across the country, has impacted air quality and the overall health and life expectancy of the Indian population dramatically. Up to 40% of children below twelve living in India's largest cities are suffering from lung diseases and other breathing illness like asthma. With the growth of its consumer economy, India has neglected its environment, and the effects of such neglect have resulted in serious environmental issues.

India's consumer economy is emulating Western economies. Owning cars and sprawl has had dramatic effects. Large swaths of agricultural lands are being converted into commercial developments, and Industrial pollutants contribute to the increase in respiratory diseases. India must prioritize the creation of a national migration policy and create firm and transparent regulations for urban development. The country's major cities need to contain urban sprawl, and limit the number of commercial complexes in these urban centers. India's continued urban development must be done with an eye for local needs and capabilities. Copying the Western model that introduces multiple cars for a single family is failing in India due to a shortage of open space. All the common land, even in the most affluent areas, has been taken over by cars parked illegally. Increased daily traffic congestion and dramatic population migration to the cities, are direct consequences of India's failure to introduce such regulations. India's urban centers are heavily polluted by the rampant increase in private automobiles, massive industrial contamination, and India's failure to enforce existing environmental laws.

In addition to government regulation and its implementation, India must work with the private sector to reduce pollutants and participate in reversing deforestation across the country. Companies should be allowed to adopt public parks, which are in need of financial resources for their upkeep. Many countries around the world have worked with the private sector to reverse deforestation and reduce pollution from their cities. Countries have introduced carbon credit systems by which a company can sell its allocated carbon emissions it is allowed to release into the air to another company as that company uses technology to reduce its own carbon emissions. City governments across the world are working with their local companies to plant trees and reduce deforestation by providing tax credits. Introduction of non-gasoline powered public transport infrastructure, reducing cars coming into cities, and alternative source power generation investment, can lead to a reduction in pollution and better air quality.

The acquisition of basic amenities like food, water, and pollution-free air is a basic right of all Indian citizens. India must first invest in helping its citizens to get food, running drinking water, and pollution-free air as a requirement for the country to even consider becoming a major twenty-first century force.

Chapter 9

Social Benefits: Build a Caring India; 1.25 Billion Strong

India has the highest levels of poverty in the world today. Estimates place more than 500 million Indians living below the poverty line, making less than 2 USD equivalent per day. For these citizens, every day is a struggle to feed and take care of their families. Within the next twenty years, India must enact policies and programs that offer short-term financial assistance, and a long-term program to provide employment to these individuals and families. These policies and programs should enable India's poor to equip themselves to earn a living in the long run, while the financial assistance would provide immediate relief in their current situation.

In order for the government to provide financial benefits to its citizens, it must begin by building a mechanism to confirm recipients' identities in addition to assuring that the benefits reach these people. The recent government programs put in place to issue identity cards and open bank accounts in recipients' names are steps in the right direction.

People currently living below the poverty line should be divided into two groups. The first group should include people who are willing and qualified to enter vocational programs in a variety of trades such as carpentry, welding, auto repair, masonry, construction, and other similar jobs. The second group would be composed of people who are unqualified for such training. This group should be made available to non-skilled labor industries such as agriculture, small-scale manufacturing, and other manual labor-intensive industries through a government-managed labor pool. Non-skilled labor pools could also be employed by creating farming co-ops managed by the private sector on government-leased land. Food grown on these co-ops can be sold through regular food markets. Such a system would provide help to millions of people living in extreme poverty. Furthermore, by providing employment, such a program will not only make them

123

productive members of society, but also add to India's GDP significantly.

Anyone with a high school education and willing to be trained should be allowed to join a two-year trade program. These programs would require students to follow attendance and performance standards. Government should invite private companies to sponsor students' training by paying for their tuition. In return, these trainees would commit to work for their sponsor company for up to two years after they graduate. Employees breaking such contract would be required to repay their training costs to the company. As a further safeguard, a national database of defaulting employees would be made accessible to ensure that such employees are not hired at other companies until they have fulfilled their commitment to their sponsoring company.

People enrolled under these programs should also be eligible to receive assistance with food coupons, free healthcare, and housing for the duration of these programs. All these benefits must be tied to individuals' commitment, attendance, and performance. Similarly, the co-op farmers would be eligible for all these benefits only if they remain productive members of the co-op.

In addition to free primary and secondary education, all children whose families are enrolled in a training program or a co-op farm should be made eligible for free lunch programs in primary and secondary schools. Attendees of these programs should also be offered free government housing for the duration of the program as long as they continue to meet the program requirements. Co-op workers should also be given free housing for the extent of their time in the co-op. All co-op programs should be a given a non-profit designation exempting the co-ops from local, state, and national taxes.

Everyone enrolled in the job training programs and working in the co-op program should be given free health care in the government-run hospitals. Under the present health-care system, everyone is allowed to use government hospitals at almost no cost. Government hospitals should be open only to those people living below the poverty line, or to government employees.

It is very ironic that free market economy and capitalistic countries like the US run large social security programs for its elderly. Social security program provides monthly cash payments to citizens over the age of sixty-five that are funded by payroll taxes on working employees and their employers. India must explore and implement a similar program to help people living below the poverty line, as well as people who pay into a social security fund once they turn sixty-five. Considering that 65% of India's population is under thirty-five years old, a small payroll tax would go a long way toward eradicating poverty from India. The young people who pay such a tax would be automatically eligible to receive social security benefits in their old age in addition to the pension and provident fund programs already available to them.

India must also focus on introducing and implementing a minimum wage to bring social justice to its masses. A fixed minimum wage allows families with full-time employees to sustain themselves, as well as forcing corporations to pay fair wages. Currently, India's minimum wage is set the 2012 rate of Rupees 17 per hour. The minimum wage should be revised annually based on inflation, and steps must be taken to enforce the payment of minimum wage by employers.

Chapter 10

It's Time to Stop India's Wasteful Subsidies

Since its independence, India's politicians have used subsidies as tactics to buy votes from different groups of people.

Subsidies to farmers in seeds, fertilizers, and power, subsidized oil and gas products, major subsidies in fares in railways and other transportation run by the government, and textiles, are a norm in India. Successive governments have spent billions to placate various groups, either to hide the incompetence of an industry as a whole or keep people employed to make sure there is no mass unrest because of high unemployment.

It is not uncommon for state governments to offer freebies such as free or subsidized rice to millions of people. It is intended to help the poor, but unfortunately these schemes increase corruption and move large amounts of money into unintended pockets. In reality, these subsidies do not go to the people it is intended to help. Most of the money is lost to corruption in the bureaucratic apparatus. It is easy to sell food products in the black market for a profit and show it was distributed to poor people. Given millions of people are without an identification card, there is really no way to confirm who ultimately benefited from the giveaway. Additionally, a large part of the subsidies go to the middle class, who are well informed and know about these subsidies before the poor, for whom the subsidies are really created, ever get to know. The simplest example of such a subsidy is cooking gas. Most middle class folks use this subsidy, whereas most poor people do not even have the resources to use cooking gas on a daily basis due to investments required in purchasing a gas stove and the subsidized gas cylinder. As people in the middle class earning much higher than the minimum wage can easily afford to pay for a gas cylinder at the market price, subsidies should only go to people living in poverty.

In some industrial sectors, it could be justified to give a subsidy to help create or grow a new industry or promote certain technology, but over time, if not curtailed, it becomes a permanent drain on taxpayers. Additionally, people get accustomed to subsidies and it becomes very

126

hard to take them away. For example, adoption of solar power by homeowners and business buildings is key for India's success. A subsidy to promote such adoption until the prices drop to a level where it becomes feasible for a large population to adopt solar power is one of the right examples of government subsidy.

Similarly, if India wants to develop its infrastructure and sustain services such as railways or other transport, all fare subsidies should be removed. Today, most of Indian Railways' infrastructure is old and prone to accidents. Indian Railways has a history of accidents in comparison to other large railway carriers in the world. For railways which transport tens of millions of people across the country on a daily basis, it should not provide any subsidy except to people living below poverty line traveling only for certain well-deserved reasons.

Today, India subsidizes healthcare for all of its citizens through its government hospitals. However, government should only provide healthcare through the government hospitals to government employees and people who are unable to afford healthcare in a private market. Based on their incomes, government employees should be eligible for free or subsidized government-funded healthcare. Additionally, people who live well below the poverty line and do not have any other way to get healthcare should be allowed to get free or subsidized healthcare from any public and private hospitals. Government must require private hospitals to provide a certain number of hours of free medical care as part of the hospital's licensing. In return for private hospitals providing free medical care to India's poor, government should give them tax breaks.

In the 2015 budget of approximately 300 billion dollars, the Indian government allocated 37 billion USD to subsidies across various industries. In the same year, India ran a 117 billion USD trade deficit (i.e. India imported goods worth 117 billion USD equivalent more than the goods it exported) with India's overall debt totaling 500 billion USD. Such subsidies end up increasing India's overall debt and hurting its economy in the long run.

India should focus on growing its industry, employment, and its tax base. Creating more jobs will necessitate fewer people looking for subsidies, thereby allowing the government to use money to provide subsidies tactically rather than as a way of life.

Chapter 11

Work Ethic - Teach it, Enforce it, or Else

Given that 65% of the Indian population is younger than thirty-five years old, one would think that the right economic policies are the only requirement to tap India's great potential. However, even in cases where policy makers attempt to institute the right economic policies, India's youth are still not receiving the required guidance necessary to compete with their international counterparts. Even if tomorrow the Indian government were able to bring 1 million manufacturing jobs to India, one could not be sure that India could find 1 million workers with the right skills to fill these positions.

Even though India lacks people with the right skills required, in reality the problem is bigger than just education. First and foremost, it is an issue of work ethic. Today, a large section of India's younger generations are prioritizing shortcuts over gaining the required knowledge or putting in the required hard work. Right through primary schools, parents want their kids to be street smart – i.e. the ability to convince others of their skills even when they are not qualified. They want their children to focus on style rather than substance. In high schools, a large number of students do not want to put in the effort to gain the knowledge, but are focused on getting good grades by any means. This could be bribing someone to get a copy of the examination paper before the exam, outright cheating by getting answers in the exam, threatening teachers or bribing them to sway their grades, or finding others to appear in exams in their place. Such practices are detailed in various newspapers in India on a daily basis. National test paper leaks are common occurrences. A severe lack of written and verbal communications skills is easily visible in hundreds of thousands of resumes posted on India's job boards. Absenteeism and lack of professionalism in entry-level job seekers is widespread. According to recruiters, over ninety percent of applicants do not show up for scheduled job interviews. A large number of applicants do not join the company even after signing a job offer.

Shorter work hours and extra leave is standard when choosing an employer. Over the last decade, a number of international companies completely stopped outsourcing in certain industries in India because of the unethical behavior of employees. One such example: the remote tech support industry initially produced hundreds of thousands of jobs with the right combination of computer literate youth working at lower labor prices than available in the US. After five years, the industry was completely shut down due to massive credit card theft and poor quality of work by the Indian workforce. Today, after India led the world in customer support call center migration from developed countries, a number of companies moved millions of call center jobs to the Philippines, Mexico, and Argentina.

Typically, in a US factory, punctuality and attendance is a key requirement. If a factory or an office is scheduled to start at 8:00 AM, every employee is present at that time. In a US office or plant, it is rare to see employees and other workers walk in a half hour late, which is fairly typical in India's work culture.

Once, in my early days in the US, I was amazed to see a student closing a college cafeteria at 11:00 PM and working his hardest to make the floors shine like new. I asked him why he was being so diligent in doing his job when there was no supervisor to watch him in the middle of the night. An okay job would do as well. He told me that he valued the quality of his work. He was doing his best not to impress anyone but to best his own satisfaction. That was the lesson that defined US workers' concept of work ethic to me.

Similarly, a college student who showed up in class half an hour before the class started at 7:30 AM every day left me with a memorable moment. I told the student that I was very impressed with her attendance, sincerity, assignment work, grades, and participation in the class. Her response was one of shock for me asking her that question. She responded that she was paying her hard-earned money to attend that class and why would she be any different? She told me that she was attending college to learn and she was making sure that she gave her best effort towards that goal. It was not to *get* a good grade. It was to *earn* a good grade.

It is very important to remember that just seventy years ago, India won its freedom from the British by following a message of truth. Mahatma Gandhi brought millions of Indians together by reminding them of the truth that the British occupation was immoral and wrong. He asked everyone to join him to ask the British to leave India, as individual freedom was a fundamental right of its people given to man by India's ancient texts.

India's foundation as a people is defined by the ***Upanishads***, which states "***Sathyam Vada; Dharmam Chara*** (Speak the Truth, pursue Righteousness)" as a way to live one's life. India's other religious text ***Puranas*** states: "***Sathayameva Jayathe*** (Truth alone triumphs)." India's history is full of heroes taking the path of truth. ***Harischandra***, who gave up his kingdom, wife, and son, and even chose to serve as a watchman in a burning-ghat, is the supreme example of one who stood for Truth. India must teach its youth what made India the envy of rest of the world in ancient times. Indians were the people who built universities in the Common Era and built successful societies based on these basic principles of truth and doing the right thing and not taking shortcuts in life.

In a well-functioning economy, it is unacceptable to take shortcuts and trick the system. A fair society cannot grow in an environment where the value of cheating for personal gain is ingrained in its younger generations. This way of thinking dilutes everything that a country should produce and stand for. Ultimately, cheating the system will produce deficient products, substandard services, and eventually a nation dominated by products from other countries. It is visible in Indian products and India's acceptance of a sub-standard for everything in daily life. India's populace accepts poor quality of food, sub-standard housing, sub-standard transport systems, and an overall poor quality of life without questioning or demanding a better alternative. In the 1980s, when Japanese products dominated the world, Japanese society was obsessed with creating quality products at the best possible price. By just following that practice, the Japanese were able to innovate and lead world markets in electronics and automobile industries. Today, Chinese companies are dominating all over the world, even in India, in selling products in every sector of the economy, producing better quality products than their counterpart in India at cheaper prices.

Additionally, India's recently deregulated education system is exacerbating the problem, as India's schools and colleges are evolving into businesses and leaving behind the tradition of teaching values and creating the next generation of scientists, policymakers, entrepreneurs, and achievers who would be responsible for advancing the nation. Public and privately funded schools and colleges go under the radar without being held responsible for producing graduates basic written and verbal communications skills. Serious citizen and government intervention is needed in setting up standards for education. India must set up national standard testing for every college for these schools to continue to be in the business of education. They must be put on probation if more than 20% of students in any grade fail the standard tests, and should be closed if they cannot improve after a warning. This is extremely serious, as without ethics and proper work ethic, India will continue to languish as a country, even if the right economic policies are introduced and implemented.

India is standing at an important juncture. In the next twenty years, India could become a formidable economy. Or India could lapse into a disappointing decline marked by a great economic divide between a few rich and an enormously large poor population—the direction India is moving today. India's fifty-seven richest people own wealth held by the bottom 70% of the population—i.e. fifty-seven people hold wealth equivalent to the bottom 950 million people combined. In the year 2000, the top 1% of rich people in India owed 36.8% of wealth. By 2017, 1% of India's rich now own 53% of India's wealth. In this worst-case scenario, India could become the worst incarnation of both capitalistic and socialistic societies, with a few rich citizens ruling the country and its poorer citizens absorbing the impact of its financial obligations. In order to become the world's next great economy, India must teach and enforce work ethic and structure to promote the right values and expunge the wrong values that are currently getting hold of India's youth.

It must begin with the parents, whose guidance is irreplaceable. Following this, teachers and school administrators at the local, state, and national level must be trained to provide quality education. Teachers and school administrators must be recognized and rewarded for their efforts to foster the right values and chastise the wrong values. India must look next to the policy makers at the local, state, and national level to ensure standards are defined and maintained, and legal systems function properly. In the present day, taking shortcuts has no consequences, and instead enables people to move up. This is a dangerous path for the nation, and India must recognize it and find ways to reverse it. The majority of the modern world's advanced countries were built on the values of fairness, hard work, and achievement instead of scraping by with mediocre work and shortcuts that will negatively affect generations to come.

Chapter 12

Population: Strength in Numbers but Resources are Limited

Within a decade, India will be the world's most populous country. India should look to its population of 1.2 billion people for strength. Large population density is not a barrier to success if the right framework is implemented so that every citizen is contributing to the country's success. Countries like Japan, South Korea, Taiwan, and Belgium have done tremendously well with similar population densities. If given the right training and resources, India's economy could be a thousand times the economy of Japan.

At the same time, India must work to control its population with the understanding that its natural resources are limited and it will eventually become impossible to supply the amounts of grain, water, and land required to support it. Family planning programs should be advertised through various channels, including educational, broadcast, and social media. The government can use primary and secondary schools to reach out to students and as parents to learn about family planning. As part of free tuition in government schools, parents may be required to attend family planning seminars and could receive assistance from a family planning counselor if needed.

Family planning must become the largest national media campaign. All media networks must be asked to donate part of their broadcast time to air these messages developed with the help of the right government agencies. All marriages must be required to be registered with the courts. Couples must be provided a family planning seminar and financial benefits as part of the marriage registration process. Marriage licenses should not be given unless the new couple has attended such a seminar. All government agencies, including those, which provide registration for childbirth, and all hospitals, must promote family planning at every opportunity, considering it is a national priority. A particular calendar month should be dedicated as "national family planning month" to spread awareness of India's need to slow down its population growth. It should be chosen based on the month the highest number of pregnancies has been recorded in previous years. During this month, government must allocate significant resources and co-ordinate with media and other key participants to spread message of family planning and methods to every corner of the country.

Government must work with all willing religious leaders to discuss and formulate a plan to slow down population growth. All religious groups willing to participate in such efforts should be allowed higher tax breaks provided they can effectively prove the results expected from the program established between the government and religious leaders.

All college students must be required to take a course on family planning. Part of the course should be to meet with ten families per academic year and give them a seminar as part of their curriculum on the benefits of and paths to family planning. College students should not be allowed to graduate unless they have completed a family planning program requirement. Students attending colleges in health and medicine programs should be required to give the family planning seminar to an increased twenty families per academic year in order to graduate from their course.

Financial benefits should be offered to all citizens to participate in family planning. A retirement allowance should be given to couples that had two children at their retirement age. Families with one child should get even a higher allowance. Government should introduce a family planning card to families with two or less children. Businesses should be encouraged to give discounts to families participating in family planning programs. Hotels, restaurants, movie theaters, and other service providers should give discounts to such families, and a special tax break could be provided to businesses showing such discounts provided to families participating in family planning programs.

India should investigate and ask in a national referendum to set a minimum marriage age for women to be raised to twenty, and men's marriage age to be raised to 23. All marriages must require the legal marriage age to be strictly followed, and all underage marriages must be prosecuted and severely fined. Additional financial rewards should be provided to couples who wait at least two years after marriage to have a child. Higher rewards should be given if the couples wait for three, four, or five years.

India must prioritize the goal of achieving zero population growth by 2050 and, to that end, should set five-year goals to reduce population growth rates. This program should be nationally funded, and quarterly and semi-annual progress reports should be reported nationally. States falling behind the national goal should be helped to achieve these goals.

Today, India is in the international spotlight, and global attention will be paid to India's actions over the next twenty years. India's citizen can either work to build India into a first-world country, or continue with our status quo and stay behind. India must identify, fund, and promote ways for India's citizens to give their best to their country. With its strength in numbers, India must find and nurture Indian talent to produce the greatest achievements in human history. At the same time, India must manage population growth to ensure there are enough resources to take care of all of its needs.

Chapter 13

End Corruption – Implement Technology, Transparency and Electoral Finance Reform

According to a recent report by Transparency International, an anti-corruption global civil society organization, India is the most corrupt country in Asia today. According to its recent survey, 70% of people in India pay a bribe to get basic public services they are entitled to receive from taxpayer-funded government organizations. Up to 54% of people had to bribe police to get them to take an action, 58% of the people had to bribe school officials, and 59% had to pay someone to get medical care from a government hospital.

Today, corruption is present wherever a citizen interacts with government employees of authority when they lack the technology to trace that interaction. Introduction of technology, and rules requiring fixed time frames for all government services, should be the first step to reduce corruption. Today, most of the time, police do not even allow citizens to file a First Incident Report (FIR), which is required for police to take any action. FIRs are only filed unless there is a serious crime or one is willing to pay a bribe. Similarly, setting a mandatory time frame to resolve a legal case will force courts to act. In the US, most police departments are now moving towards body cameras for police to be held accountable. Most police cars already have a camera recording all traffic violation stops, or other actions taken by the police. All courts are required by law to get a case decision in a certain time frame.

Furthermore, as discussed earlier, the best way to reduce corruption in citizens' day-to-day life is to outsource services to private organizations (except the key required functions of the government), which deal directly with day-to-day services. Banks, airlines, state transport, railways, and medical services are a few such services that must be privatized. No one pays a bribe in a private hospital or a bus run by a private organization. At the same time, all government workings should be made transparent by use of technology so government officials cannot take bribes to give out a new license for a bus route or just deny action towards a genuine complaint.

Today one of the biggest sources of corruption in India is the funding of its political system. Most politicians have accumulated wealth far beyond what their government compensation enables them to accumulate. Most of this wealth is gained from "party funds." Party funds are created when a political party comes to power. When a party's proposed development projects are approved, or a prior approved project gets funded, a percentage of the funds are siphoned into party coffers to fund future political activity. A small cut of the funds is designated for the government department employees executing the project, and the remainder of the funds is passed up the hierarchy. In the end, the percentage of money assigned to a government-funded project is delivered to the minister running that department.

Such party funds are the root cause of systematic big corruption in India. In order to remove such corruption, in addition to contracting out all these services to private industry, a legal and transparent channel to raise money for political candidates to contest elections must be made available.

India's political campaign financial system is severely flawed. As per the election campaign laws, a person is allowed to spend up to 115,000 USD equivalent on political campaigning, where as per the political parties and other published sources, it takes twenty to thirty times more money to contest and be a competitive candidate in an Indian election. Most of this money is spent off the books from unlisted sources. With corporations now allowed to give as much money as they want to politicians legally, it has further worsened the politician-businessman connection. Earlier political parties received backing from businesses to fund election expenses mostly off the books, and in return businesses received favors, such as government contracts and large loans from public banks with a wink from politicians. With making these donations legal, the whole political process is now further weakened, making it impossible to break the cycle of corruption. India must reform its campaign financing system, barring companies from making direct contributions to politicians or political parties.

The whole political fundraising and spending process must be reviewed and made transparent. To achieve this, any and all sources of funds in a political party must be clearly provided to the election commission. In the case of a willful irregularity, the candidate should be automatically disqualified and removed from the election process or from the elected position. Furthermore, India must invest in technology and personnel to make sure that the pre and post election process is robust. To this end, qualified candidates from certified local and national parties should be given the financial support required to contest an election, in addition to being allowed to raise money so long as every cent is properly declared for every constituent to see. This same public process should be set up to show all election expenses by the candidates. If India can be an international back office for the world, it can surely build a transparent system to audit funds raised and spent for the several thousand campaigning candidates during election years.

This process must continue to be in effect even after the election is over, because as soon as a candidate is elected, they will have an increased ability to get money from businesses and individuals they regulate. A government without a fair process to contest and elect people's representatives is merely an autocracy in the clothes of a democracy. If India's elected representatives are not fit to represent the people and do not have the people's interest at heart, then the idea of an Indian democracy is not what was envisioned by India's founding fathers.

Today, India's politicians are some of the richest people without much success in education, business, or inheritance. All candidates elected for public office and all government employees must declare their public assets, including all assets in the name of their spouses and children. Assets from all elected officials and direct relations and government employees should be declared every year for the public to know they are not accumulating assets by illegal means. Banks should be mandated to report any deposits larger than ten percent of their salaries to an anti-corruption department. Such a department should be independent, with its head reporting to the prime minister's or chief minister's offices. The exiting prime minister at the national —and the exiting chief minister for the state level—elections should also appoint the heads of department for the next election for a one-time five-year term. All cases of corruption should be reported and dealt with in a special court focused on corruption.

Today, it is easy for a tax department to threaten a company with an audit and make it go away with a bribe. Government must invest heavily in India's tax department in technology and personnel to audit the tax returns of all small, medium, and large businesses. All retail businesses must be required to issue receipts. Businesses must be mandated to use cash registers for all transactions, and be able to produce an electronic history of all transactions to audit their sales. Today, government loses billions of USD equivalent in income tax, as most businesses are able to manipulate their revenues through cash sales and avoid paying taxes on their total income. This money is then used in enabling a parallel cash economy. This large parallel cash economy has allowed a black market to thrive and money to be hidden from banks and auditable transactions. Additionally, it has created a huge imbalance of wealth in Indian society.

To counter this imbalance, government should outsource development and integration of all real estate, banking, and other large asset transaction systems to track the movement of large sums of money based on PAN cards and other personal identifications issued by the government. Laws could be created that all payments over Rupees 5,000 can only be made by a check or electronic transfer. Government itself should start making all purchases and payments via electronic means. All companies doing business with local, state, and national government must receive payments through electronic means.

It is interesting to note that most people working in the government, if given a choice, would rather not be involved in corruption. Most of the corruption in the government is either demanded by the people in authority or almost due to the low compensation provided in government jobs. Once transparency and major electoral finance reform is introduced, it will reduce top-down corruption significantly. At the same time, people will move out of dead-end, low-paying government jobs to higher-paying private sector jobs that have the possibility of moving higher in the organization based on their qualifications and effort.

To counter corruption, departments like Vigilance should work closely with agencies in charge of implementing technology for every government process to bring transparency and reduce corruption across city, state, and national governments. Monitoring communications between government employees over government-issued emails, making all government contracting transparent, and moving government from a seniority-based promotion system to a performance-based system, is a few examples where implementation of technology can increase productivity and reduce corruption significantly.

Lastly, India still lags the world in terms of ease of doing business. The experience of starting a new business can be a cumbersome and painful process to go through. Currently, it can be fast-tracked by bribing the officials responsible for issuing the required paperwork. The fast track should be made a legitimate option for a higher payment by the individual. Then all such money will go to the government rather than as a bribe. As discussed before, time lines for all government services will further eliminate opportunities of corruption at various government departments. Local, state, and national governments must look at all such processes and set time lines for all government deliverables in consultation with various government agencies.

Chapter 14

Equality: Demand and Enforce it!

Every successful democracy around the world stands on two basic principles: freedom of speech, and the equality of all citizens. For India to become a leading and successful democracy rather than just another democracy in the running, both facts are not only to be believed but also to be practiced in real life.

India is still fighting nineteenth-century discrimination based on caste, religion, and treating women as second-class citizens. Reservations based on caste in education and jobs is hurting India. India's reservation system often enables unqualified people to be put in positions that may decide the fate of India's future generations. A nation is only as good as its leaders. In war, a country does not send its old and the weak. In a crisis, you do not send the inexperienced to resolve the situation. So to lead the nation, India needs its best and brightest and not the most repressed in leadership positions. India needs to make sure that all forms of repressions are tackled head-on by enforcing laws to treat everyone equally and fairly.

Millions of India's people have been repressed and discriminated against for centuries, and continue to be discriminated against today. India must provide financial incentives to people who need help to make the playing field level for everyone. Allowing all children to have same level of education is allowing a level field for everyone. In the US, every child, irrespective of its religion, national origin, and income level, attends the same public school and are afforded the same opportunities throughout primary and secondary education. India must enact severe punishments for schools, companies, and individuals found to promote discrimination.

Reservations in their current form have created more division in society than benefits overall. India's reservations in government jobs were enacted for the ten years after India gained independence from the British. Since then, reservations in education and jobs have been used as a political tool to gain votes by dividing people on the basis of caste. In its current form, reservations have become a birthright of a very few, whose parents or grandparents have already benefited from such a program in the past. Their children, being better off than others, have a chokehold on such benefits. As a result, India's current reservation policies do not even help the wide range of people these reservations are meant to. Reservations should be replaced with financial assistance for all, and harsh penalties must be levied against people participating in discrimination, especially based on caste.

On the same lines of equal rights and participation, all citizens should be bound to one legal code. Law is based on human empathy and treats everyone with equal respect. A country cannot pass laws that discriminate or benefit one group of people over another, based on religion or caste. Any laws that allow people to be treated differently based on their caste or religion will enable people to find ways to use these laws to divide and exploit people. There are political parties who have successfully built their identities and have been elected to govern India who have openly stood for the promotion of a caste of people or a religion. Such identification of political parties based on caste, religion, or regional identity should be unconstitutional.

India has to learn from other successful democracies to keep state and religious matters separate. Every citizen is allowed to follow the faith they choose in the privacy of their homes and the temple, church, and mosque, in which they choose to worship. But the government must be free of any and all religious beliefs and preferences. Government must enforce one law equal to all of a secular nation. Given India's diversity, India's government must treat all religions equally. India cannot afford such divisions. India is a melting pot of religions, languages, belief systems, and diversity of ideas like the US is a melting pot of races and cultures. The US has created a model to achieve success in every realm of life. By accepting everyone equally without the consideration of his or her religion, caste, or background, India can also achieve unimaginable success. Dividing its people on the basis of religion, language, and region, is a downward spiral India cannot afford to take.

Over the last thirty years, Indian women have made significant progress in women's rights. Women have entered all kinds of professional fields and sports, and have succeeded in every sphere of life. It is time India's laws are enforced to treat women as equal to men, and provide them with equal opportunities and compensation in all fields. In a country where infanticide of girls still happens in the twenty-first century, and women are killed even today in the name of dowry, India has to look at equality for women as one of the main national issues for India to become a leading nation in the world in the twenty-first century.

Crimes against women have become a common occurrence. Stories of rape, murder, and burning in India are heard across the world too frequently. Laws should be made stricter for such heinous offenses and must be strictly implemented. Offenses involving anyone found guilty of dealing with child brides and infanticides must carry life sentences and death penalties. High school education among girls should be mandatory. Such education must be further promoted through scholarships, work-study programs, and other financial means. Law must punish parents or guardians forcing girls to work and not allowing them to attend school. India must set a goal of 100% high school education for girls by 2030.

India is one of the unique countries where diverse group of people have come together to form a country, unlike continents like Europe where people following the same religion and with same ancestry have fought over the centuries and have created separate countries. It is amazing that even though people speak different languages, different clothes, worship different gods, and even have different cuisine, they serve the same country. Together, unity in diversity is India's biggest strength. India must preserve this unity at all cost. There is no place for regionalism and it must act in the strongest ways to overcome the ideas and people who may want to divide it based on its diversity. Only together can India be the biggest exporter of space, automotive, telecommunications, and automotive technology in the twenty-first century. Only together can it create a million-person-strong army. Only together can it be the largest economy in the world in the twenty-first century. By breaking it apart, Indian states will get back to the cycle of fighting with each other as one part becomes stronger than its neighbor.

India has achieved incredible integration of races, religions, and people towards one cause of building a better tomorrow. If India proceeds with the required reforms, India will become the envy of its neighbors and the whole world. India has the youth, numbers, intellect, and history to be the best in the world. It has come too far to turn back to inequality and division based on caste, religion, and regionalism. For India to become one of the world's leading countries, equality of men and women, protection of all citizens under one law, and elimination of discrimination based on caste, religion, and all other means, must be demanded and enforced.

Chapter 15

India's Message to the World and its Foreign Policy

Since its independence from the British, India has prided itself as a country with an independent mindset. It has always stood up for the right thing without acting as a proxy of powerful countries on the world stage. Such a national policy of non-alignment at the international level has not only helped India gain respect from its peers but also avoid getting drawn into global or regional conflicts. It has further allowed India to pick its relationships based on its needs versus ideologies promoted by Western or Eastern countries. Given India's independent stance has worked well for the last seventy years, India must stay firm on that course. At the same time, India must speak up on issues to create its own identity boldly in the world. As India has been a secular and democratic state since its existence as a sovereign country, India must speak up to provide an independent voice to the world on issues of democracy, human rights, and the independence of each country.

In the twenty-first century, looking at all the models of government, it is very clear that a democratic state managed by its elected officials, with laws approved by a majority of its population, a market economy allowed to run efficiently, and a social system helping the poor to rebuild a dignified life, is the best way to build a successful society. India must promote such values as its message to the world. Additionally, India should share its history and its way of life as described in its ancient texts over thousands of years of Indian civilization.

India must strengthen its role at the United Nations to support weaker countries, speak out against dictators, and against powerful countries when they act unilaterally against smaller countries or prop up dictators for their own benefits. At the same time, India should stand firm for the protection of human rights. Given India today has a much larger percentage of people, it must ask for a greater role in the United Nations, including a permanent seat in the UN's security council, and veto power like its other five members: UK, US, Russia, China, and France.

As a foreign policy interest, India must lead in supporting a policy of reduction in the arms race, especially nuclear arms and the protection of the environment. Currently, India is spending a significant amount of its GDP in arming its defense forces, as South East Asia has become one of the most armed regions in the world. India must become a leading voice in reducing arms. These resources must be directed towards bettering the environment and reducing poverty around the world.

India should lead within the United Nations' charter to create an alliance similar to NATO that could protect developing nations of this alliance from a military or terrorist attack. Each nation in the alliance would contribute their men, women, and funds towards the creation of an international force for protection of all of its member states. It would help reduce the unlimited money spent in stockpiling arms and taking money away from urgent issues in poor and developing countries.

India should lead by example, protecting its own environment by moving away from fossil fuels and implementing power generation by solar power, building renewable power public transport, and reversing deforestation, while asking other nations to follow its lead. India must remind the world that developed nations have been largely responsible for the increasingly high CO2 levels on Earth over the last hundred years, and must contribute by helping smaller countries to move away from a carbon economy. Developed countries should not only reduce CO2 levels, as they are still the largest contributors of CO2, they should help developing and poor countries financially move to renewable sources of energy.

Like any other sovereign nation, India's foreign policy should be focused on promoting and protecting its self-interests. Trade agreements supporting exports of Indian products and the import of products India needs for day-to-day life should be the basis of its foreign policies.

Promotion of tourism to India and mutual visa-free travel treaties with other countries must be explored, as this will help India communicate its message of peace and its way of life to the world. India's foreign policy should be focused on extending trade between India and other countries, including services such as software development, medical tourism, exchange of college students, opening India's universities to other countries, and helping other developing nations with technological exchanges.

India, given its past, must speak out against occupation of other nation states. India should provide a leading voice for true freedom of people in Palestine, and stand with people against ethnic genocide, such as happened in Rwanda or Kosovo or Burma, or in other parts of the world in the future. India, with its history of occupation by Mughals, or the British, for over a thousand years, has a responsibility to speak up against all kind of occupation even if it hurts India's self-interests.

Lastly, India should take a position that promotes a certain percentage of the GDP from developed and developing countries is set aside in an international fund to help countries in need through food programs, promotion of literacy, election monitoring, micro-banking, protection of human rights, and equality at all levels.

Chapter 16

Last Word

It was a conversation with a taxi driver over a long drive that kept the idea of writing ***Waiting For Us | For the India We Deserve*** alive with me for over a decade. I posed a question that if the solution of India's problems was to elect India's educated, accomplished, and concerned citizens, would you vote for them? I offered myself as an imaginary candidate, someone educated who grew up in India knowing the daily grinds of life, knowing India can only be changed by a set of policy implementations, willing to take the step to change the lives of India's future generations.

His first answer was not if he would vote for such a candidate. His kind suggestion was not to even try. In his opinion, the existing political class would eat up India's well-meaning citizens before they even had a chance. To his bewilderment, if you were educated and found a way to make a professional living, why would you want to associate yourself with such a vile profession? He was sure that India's well-meaning, educated youth did not stand a chance.

What stayed with me for all these years was his parting suggestion that even though he might not vote for a candidate like me, he would very much want someone to try. So writing ***Waiting For Us*** is a first step to get on that path to try to bring millions of people together to bring the change India deserves.

India today has come a long way from being a collection of smaller countries ruled by dictators, and then ruled by Mughals and the British. India has a lot of positives going for it as a nation. It has thriving democratic institutions, a large number of universities, a market economy, a large banking system spread across the country, and a young population expected to take India to top of the world in the twenty-first century. India is blessed with a distinguished cultural history, detailing how to make the best of one's life and build a great society. Its historical books teach one how to live a perfect family life, and how to be successful with dedication and hard work. India's scientists, engineers, doctors, and blue-collar workers are known around the world for their intellect and hard work.

With all these positives, countries around the world consider India to be a bright spot with a lot of hope and expectations. India is expected to become one of the largest economies in the next thirty years. Since the origins of Hinduism almost five thousand years ago, it is really the first time that India has had the opportunity to apply its knowledge of building a just and prosperous society described such as "Ram Raj" in its holy books. With the right political will and its over one-billion-strong population, India can create a nation that can be envy of the world. With guidance from India's religious texts of creating a great society and solutions from across the world to solve day-to-day problems, the right policy framework can build India into an example of success in the world.

But at the same time, India stands at a critical juncture. India has to tackle major challenges. With its large population, India faces significant social, economic, environmental, and critical resource challenges required to feed, house, train, employ, and manage its people. Any one of these spheres of life can become a major obstacle for India's vision. As discussed in the book, a few consecutive poor rainfall seasons can create catastrophic famine in the country; lack of hygiene and failure to control human generated waste can turn into a disease epidemic; lack of a good education system can continue to increase unemployment to dangerous levels; high unemployment can turn into out-of-control increase in crime; and illiteracy can continue to feed into higher population growth. All these issues are circular and inter-related. Failure in one of these issues can create a domino effect ending in catastrophic failure.

My intent in writing this book is to raise the urgency for India's leaders at every level to tackle these problems now, to implement solutions to resolve them before it is too late. Failure to recognize and solve these issues will take India back to where India started. If India is not able to control its population, unable to feed its people, provide drinking water to all, jobs to its youth, reduce the income gap between its rich and poor, and reverse its environmental decay, India will see a rise in regionalism, and over time states may ask to leave the union to solve the same issues locally in a state. In the end, the failure of solving these issues will take India back to where it was a thousand years ago, a warring set of states focused on short-term local gain, and ultimately another thousand-year rule by another outsider.

India must control its population growth; build political systems that promote innovation and reward its most productive individuals; remove government from running industry; build an efficient and fair judicial system, which works in weeks and months rather than years; build infrastructure so industry can thrive; create transparency to abolish corruption; reform its education system to compete with the best in the world; remove reservations at every aspect of life so India's best and brightest are allowed to lead the nation; and get ahead of its most urgent environmental problems to join the ranks of developed countries around the world.

It is my hope that, at the least, ***Waiting For Us*** is able to identify the root causes of India's problems faced by its average citizens in their day-to-day life, and offers a framework for India's current and next generation of leaders to look at these problems from a policy perspective. With implementation of such a framework, India can not only become the largest economy in the world, but also lead the world by sharing its human values to live happy and meaningful lives.

The most successful outcome would be for ***Waiting For Us*** to become the policy guide for similar-minded youth to come together under a platform to organize politically and make India ***what we deserve***!